# YOU SELLING YOU

# BY

# STEVE MILLER

Published 2006 by arima publishing

www.arimapublishing.com

ISBN 1-84549-093-2

© Steve Miller 2006

Printed and bound in the United Kingdom

Typeset in Verdana 11/16

arima publishing
ASK House, Northgate Avenue
Bury St Edmunds, Suffolk IP32 6BB
t: (+44) 01284 700321

www.arimapublishing.com

# CONTENTS

the difference is me ...

# PREFACE

In the year 2000, I fulfilled an important dream of mine: I became Managing Director of my own Training Organisation.

My starting point in life was no different from thousands of others; I was brought up in North Warwickshire in a working class environment where I attended the local comprehensive school. I worked hard and moved on to higher education. Since then, I've had a varied career. My first job was in holiday entertainment – it was an excellent opportunity to develop my communication and social skills. I then moved into the sales and tele-marketing business. I wanted to progress and made sure I did my job in a way I got noticed: soon I became responsible for customer service and business development. From thereon, my career continued on the up; I looked for openings that would enhance my skills, knowledge and personal profile. I worked for a number of organisations including the Rank Leisure Group and Trader Media Group where I eventually headed up the Training and Development function.

I was always mindful of my dream of starting my own successful business and I was always hungry for new ideas, new contacts and personal development. During these years, whilst working for others, I undertook professional training in Clinical Hypnosis, Executive Coaching and I took a keen interest in Emotional Intelligence, reading everything I could get my hands on about the subject. I was particularly interested in its application to leadership, sales, customer service and business development. This attention to personal progress eventually gave me the confidence, skills and knowledge to start my own Training Organisation – why not? I was now one of the experts in this field. As well as this, I also run an Executive Coaching practice which incorporates the use of Clinical Hypnosis. Further details of this can be found at **www.hypnobest.co.uk**

I currently work with a wide range of organisations specialising in the media and publishing sector and have established a reputation of having a flamboyant, practical and no nonsense style.

The techniques I describe in this book have helped me to springboard my own career and to achieve the goal of running my own successful company. I want to share these ideas with others who are ready.

My personal mission: both in running my business and in writing this book is:

**TO BUILD A WORLD OF WINNERS.**

From the outset, my aim has been to provide the tools that will support individuals in their quest to achieve their best – both for themselves and for their organisations.

Before embarking on the book, I met with a wide range of successful professionals, including entrepreneurs, executives, actors, teachers and sales professionals, to identify what it was that had helped them achieve success. I am convinced that the same lessons and ideas apply, regardless of the field of operation, regardless of whether that success is exhibited in the boardroom, the classroom or on the stage.

It is my belief that we need to consider two distinct parts responsible for personal success: the **inner** variables and the **outer** variables. As you work your way through the book, you will notice that several of the protocols suggested are aligned to the application of hypnosis; it is my whole-hearted belief that we need to groom the **inner** self first and the tools afforded by hypnosis are the most effective and powerful I have come across for this job.

During your journey through this book, you will be challenged at times – stick with it. You will find you are offered a toolkit of techniques that will be of use not just for the period of reading, but which you will be able to dip into and utilise for as far into the future as you wish.

So, smile and enjoy what could be the start of many good things to come.

Steve Miller
Birmingham, England
February 2006

# ACKNOWLEDGEMENTS

*My family for doing their best and believing in me*
*Ursula James for her great support*
*Michael Joseph for his wonderful college*
*Jean Wilde for being with me all the way*
*Alan Possart for his patience and love*
*Terry Brookes for his unconditional love and support*
*Lindsey Gibson for her incredible focus*
*My business team for their hard work*
*All of my clients for making it possible*
*All of my friends for their humour, support and patience*

# INTRODUCTION

# WHAT IS THE
## *YOU*
## *SELLING*
## *YOU*
## *PROGRAMME?*

# THE WHYS AND WHATS OF YOU SELLING YOU

**WHY...**

...should you become sold on the *You Selling You* concept?

Have you ever envied someone else's success? If you're like me, the answer is probably "yes." Envy isn't a pleasant emotion, but it is one we've all experienced. How do you deal with it? Do you let it depress you and fill you with self-pity? Do you hear yourself asking, "Why can't I have that? Why does it never work out for me?" Or is it the spur that urges you on to own success? Do you say, "That's what I want and I'm going to make it happen." It's fairly clear which response most of us would like to be able to make, but even then you may be thinking, HOW do I make it happen?

First answer the following questions honestly:
Do you want success?
Do you want to live your dreams?
Do you want to be one of life's winners?

You would think that anyone in their right mind would shout a resounding, "Yes! Yes! Yes!" (and isn't that a response we all like to hear.) Strange though it may seem, however, sometimes our response is half-hearted, unsure, and rather timid. So go ahead, and ask yourself those questions now.

How do you feel when you answer? Confident, clear and determined? Can you allow yourself to be successful?

If **your** answer to these questions is clearly, "YES," then buy into the *You Selling You* idea. This is the programme that will help you discover HOW you make that success happen. You don't wait for "it" to happen; you don't leave your progress to chance; instead, you take active steps to ensure your life's direction is the one you desire. You become the hero of your own drama, rather than the supporting role or a walk on extra.

But don't worry if you didn't feel wholly confident when you asked yourself those questions: maybe you thought "yes, I'd like to be a winner, but…" and in those "buts" there were reservations and doubts. Making a commitment to follow the exercises suggested in the *You Selling You Programme*, can help you rid yourself of those debilitating "buts…" once and for all.

> *I am always doing that which I cannot do, in order that I may learn how to do it:* Pablo Picasso.

In the following pages, I want to take you on a journey. I want to help you discover the path that will lead to a more positive you, a more confident you – to you as a

## WINNER!

## <u>The Fittest Reap the Rewards.</u>

An old saying that may sound unfair but, based on my experience of supporting people from all walks of life who had different goals and dreams, I believe it to be true. So, if you want to be one of those seemingly lucky people who get what they want and plenty of it the answer is easy: make sure that you become one of the fittest.

Being one of the fittest means you provide the right response to a number of events that require you to sell yourself.

Remember: Events + Response = Outcome.

The exercises in this book will be your work out; they will get you into shape; they will help you become the best you can, a product you're proud to sell.

Sell - That is the key.

Before I "sold" myself I rarely enjoyed promotion, material gain, acknowledgement from peers and superiors. Once I had taken myself on the journey that I outline in this book all that changed. I learned the importance of selling myself, and how to sell myself. It's a journey that hasn't just worked for me, but for many professional people I have worked with.

---

Jenny ...

... a HR Director in her mid 30s explained to me that **selling** herself was a pre-requisite of her influence as a high flying executive. Understanding this concept has meant promotion has come swiftly for her and in 8 years she has progressed from a junior P.A. to senior Human Resources Director with over 12,000 employees ... and she's still moving up.

---

What accelerated her success? What can accelerate your success? What is it that makes "that difference"?

Well first, you need to shed any inhibitions you may have about yourself as a successful person. You need to believe in yourself in order to sell yourself. You also need all round fitness. By that I don't just mean going to the gym three times a week and eating healthily, although that can be part of it. All round fitness means being in peak condition in every aspect of our make-up: yes the physical, but also the mental and emotional.

So a key part of the *You Selling You Programme* is to be the best you can.

After all, you can't really get the best price for a second rate product.

> Sow – grow and then reap the benefits:
> You are your own product.
> Grow yourself ...
> Nurture and feed yourself...

Carrying out my recommended exercises will show you how and it won't be long before you begin to notice a difference.

Others will begin to treat you with the respect and confidence that you have decided to give yourself. Soon you will be equipped to succeed in today's environment.

Organisations are increasingly searching for talent not based upon technical skills alone. They are also looking for the "difference" factor, call it the X–factor if you must, but it's the difference that they'll discover in you. Employers who are my clients often tell me of their desire to seek out those who shine. Those who have self-belief, are comfortable with themselves, who possess emotional intelligence, who exude energy and project a persona of success.

## BE ONE OF THOSE WHO SHINE.

### The New World Demands It.

The world continues to get more competitive. In business, customers have more choice and so do employers. Over the last 5 years, whilst observing successful senior managers, directors, consultants and sales professionals I have noticed that a key characteristic they all share is the ability to sell themselves to their customers, peers, directors and shareholders.

David ...
... is a 23 year old Senior Sales Executive in IT.
David was finding his results flat, mediocre and uninspiring... nothing to sing about. They were results which made him doubt himself. When I worked with him, he explained how he felt it was to do with his own anxiety and his inability to sell himself in a comfortable manner. He had already instinctively realised that his key development need was to learn to sell himself. He knew that once he could sell himself, then sales of his product would improve.

> After 6 weeks, supporting his development and helping him to learn how to sell himself, using the techniques described in this book, he became one of his company's top sales executives. Not only that, I took a call from him where he explained to me with delight how he'd sold a half million pound contract to NATO.

David is not an isolated case; he didn't just have a lucky break.

**90%**

of successful sales professionals have explained to me that their success depends upon them selling themselves first.

Businesses striving to achieve double digit profit growth know this and that the way to succeed and improve sales targets is to grow a pool of leading edge employees. This aim has appeared as a priority on the business plans of such enlightened companies.

Can you be one of those leading edge employees they're looking for? Maybe you are already at a senior level and want to engage further in corporate ladder climbing. Maybe you are employed in a role that requires you to be one of the best.

For you to join this world of winners, take responsibility and act by following the guidance I offer in this book.

> *I am not afraid of storms, for I am learning to sail my ship*: Louisa May Alcott

## People buy you ... or not.

Just for a moment, dream of one of your goals - a realistic goal. Maybe it's the job you strive for, an increase in your wealth, a new business you have in mind for the years ahead or even a dream relationship. Can you see yourself achieving this goal or will it always stay in the land of wishful thinking? Can you believe in your success? Do you believe you're good enough, that you deserve it? A colleague of mine, Jean, told me a long time ago, that people needed to believe in themselves first and when they did the rewards flowed. My own experience bears this out.

---

Steve...

...I remember the last organisation I joined before I decided to set up my own business. I enjoyed far more accelerated promotion there, than I had ever experienced previously, moving from middle management to senior management to assistant director in 3 years. This was down to my newfound ability **to sell me.** My ability to grow my own business has also been very much about selling myself. But I couldn't have sold myself well, if I hadn't believed in myself.

---

## **Believe in Yourself.**

Let's take, for an example, a leader in business implementing change. The change in question is a relocation of the workforce. The relocation is only 8 miles away, but naturally some employees will be unhappy. They enjoy working where they are and won't relish the idea of the move. Many people just don't like the idea of change, whatever it is, and however major it is.

Close your eyes and picture our first role model: Manager James is afraid of delivering the change. He appears apologetic. His body language is hunched and negative. His voice is thin and hesitant. As a member of the workforce you wonder if you are being listened to and understood.

Now picture our second role model: Manager Elaine's posture is upright. She appears to be confident and comfortable. Her voice is steady and clear. There is an energy and vibrancy about her. She inspires faith. She listens to you and remains focused.

As you imagine these two very different leaders, hear, see and feel the difference.

Imagine you are one of the workforce and on the receiving end of James' message. Then, imagine you are one of the workforce and on the receiving end of Elaine's message. Now, imagine you are James delivering the change and finally, imagine you are Elaine delivering the change.

Notice how you feel in each case: notice the difference in your physiology.

I hardly need ask the question which of our models was preferable. Who you'd prefer to work for, whether you'd be more open to the organisational change if delivered by James or Elaine. Neither is it really necessary to ask you whether you'd prefer to be able to deliver your message in the manner of James or Elaine. One way was clearly more rewarding, more comfortable.

Should you choose to follow the journey in my book, you will ensure that it is Elaine's model that you will follow. You will begin to exude confidence, inspire trust and be able to sell products, ideas, and change, because you will learn to sell yourself.

---

*The pessimist sees difficulty in every opportunity. The optimist sees the opportunity in every difficulty*:
Winston Churchill

---

Now let's take the sales executive:
Over the years, I have concluded that Pareto's 80/20 rule can be applied in driving client deals. 20% of the sale is to do with the product or service. The rest is to do with you. The pay off happens when you've got 80% of selling yourself right. Selling yourself will help you to exceed your

commercial targets and to achieve your objectives. What's more, your powers of negotiation, whether it be your salary increase, dealing with a difficult client or negotiating for what you want in non-business situations will become easier.

> Success is
> 80% selling yourself
> 20% selling your "product"

## You Deserve It.

It has taken me years of personal experience to learn how to sell myself correctly in order for me to take advantage of opportunities that have come my way and to create opportunities to bring out the best in me.

This wasn't easy. I had a big label attached to me. My label said that I was from a working class background; that my mother was a cleaner, my father an oil terminal operator. With this background, how could I possibly be successful in business? My label defined me in a particular way. I discovered it was a label I'd attached to myself, but I also began to discover I could untie the label, change it to something more in keeping with my ideas of who I really was now.

Whatever labels we parade, they tend to be difficult to shift. We tied them on tightly and as you know, the longer a knot is left, the more difficult it can be to untie. We get so used to the label, that we forget it's there, but forgetting it doesn't diminish its power. We become conditioned to see ourselves in a narrow way, to expect only so much of ourselves. Our perception of ourselves becomes dis-empowering and limiting. We accept the labels and their limitations that our environments and upbringings have embedded deep into our minds.

## **Wonderful News.**

We can remove those labels with their restrictions. We can change and make ourselves a saleable commodity. We can buy into the life we want.

It is completely possible that you become a quality product, one that never gets marked down and ends up in the bargain bin.

So to start, consider the following:

### **How kind are you on yourself?**

I want you to start thinking how kind you allow yourself to be to you. Below you will find questions that will help you assess where you are in relation to this.

Space has been provided beneath the questions so that you can record your work in progress.

---

Think carefully on each of the following questions.
Provide **1 answer only** to each question.

1. Why is the *You Selling You* concept a crucial element in achieving your life/work goal?

2. What will be the results of *You Selling You?*

3. How will you enjoy your newfound success through *You Selling You?*

4. Who will you share the *You Selling You* concept with?

5. Are you prepared to work hard and follow my journey?

---

By reflecting on these questions, you will now have an idea of what you want and why you are interested in this programme, but you may be wondering:

**WHAT...**
...is involved in buying into the *You Selling You* concept?

So let's take a look at what the **magic formula** of *You Selling You* is.

We will need to consider the key areas described below and acknowledge that these all interrelate. Each key area is like a piece of the *You Selling You* jigsaw – and you will need each piece in order to complete the picture. These areas are explored in depth later in the book and provide you with specific actions that you can undertake and which will enable you to complete the *You Selling You* picture.

## **A word about YOUR Motivation.**

Before you embark on the *You Selling You* programme, don't forget that no one, other than yourself can make you start it, stick with it and finish it. Maybe you feel that it takes such a lot of effort to motivate yourself and after all, how do you know it will be worth it?

## **TRUST ME.**

Time spent on you will mean that you will reap the rewards. What have you got to lose? The good thing about success is that it encourages further success and soon you will find that motivating yourself is no longer such a problem or effort.

I want you to consider the following points. You may find some rather hard messages contained within them, but they are for your benefit.

**I DON'T WANT YOU TO READ ON UNTIL YOU FEEL YOU CAN ACCEPT THEM.**

a) Are you living a "victim life"? What I mean by that is: are you the sort of person who has an internal dialogue that includes phrases like, "Why me?" "It's alright for them." "I could never be as good as that." "I couldn't do that." And do you ever hear yourself saying, "It's not fair?"

This kind of inner speak often leads us to put others down, to disparage their successes in order to make us feel better; we displace our jealousy and sense of inadequacy by trying to undermine others.

b) Are you an "I can't be bothered" type? People who live with this attitude often find themselves becoming "fat" in body and mind. Exercising and using the "muscle" of the mind is crucial to the success of you selling you. Often this type feels lethargic and bored and they become trapped in a tedious cycle of sluggishness. And it's all down to laziness. For example, how many "diets" have you read about, maybe started, possibly finished, but then found the weight piling back on? This type may put in a bit of effort, for a while, but then don't sustain it. It is those individuals who take **a personal responsibility** for their own lives; those who become **bothered,** who become the real "weight loss successes." Those who fail ultimately have never taken on this responsibility, they have assumed buying a diet book, following a few instructions for a period of time will help them succeed, but they give responsibility over to the diet rather than take it upon themselves. And of course, this principle applies to all other areas of success – not just weight loss. Remember we can get fat in the mind as well as the body!

c) Are you a "yes, but" type? In a way this is a sort of a/b type combo. Unlike a-types the c-type does have a more positive inner dialogue, to start with: they do think they "can do it." Also, unlike the b-type, they do get up off their backsides and are ready to take action BUT, it is at this stage that they fall. They begin to doubt. Their inner dialogue contains phrases such as; "I might come across as too arrogant, too cocky, too confident … etc…" In a way this is a kind of escape hatch. These types, when it comes to taking real action, are not willing to give themselves fully to whatever venture it is that would take them beyond their present state. They are unable to release the saleable part of themselves. And why? Because, they are not willing to step out of their comfort zone. They can't or won't search for what is really inside of them. They need to take heed of that wonderful M People song: "You Gotta Search for the Hero Inside Yourself."

A Theatre Director friend of mine sees a fair few of these types: those who want it, but at the last hurdle don't sell themselves. At auditions for roles, there is stiff competition, but it is the ones who can get beyond the doubts, those who don't apologise for being there, who will make the most impact.

## Being Aware of Prolonged Low Motivation.

It is important that you acknowledge to yourself if you are stuck in a trough of low motivation. It is crucial that you are aware of the effects of such a state and take action now to change it.

With prolonged low motivation:

- You don't move forward, but stay static. It's a bit like a nasty, stubborn bacteria that takes hold of us and when we have "got it," we need a pretty strong medicine to shift it.

- If you have children, you're setting them a bad example. You are their role model don't forget.

- You limit your material wealth and gain. When you are stuck with low motivation, you are unable to drive your career and ambitions forward and limit your potential to achieve hard results.

Often, my focus when delivering leadership, negotiation and sales training, focuses on our ability to take control of our own motivation and **to get hungry.**

- You harm personal relationships. Who wants to come home to someone who "can't be bothered." Someone who doesn't make an effort with how they look, who has no vision for the future, who has no get up and go.

- You frustrate other people. I remember my coach emphasising the importance of surrounding myself with people who energised my thinking. She described two types of people:

Radiators: those who radiate energy and fill us with enthusiasm and life.

Drains: those who seem to suck all the life out of us.

Frustrating others can lead to loss of friendships and isolation.

- You harm business relationships. I remember supporting a number of business executives responsible for generating strong customer relationships; my analysis showed that those who failed to connect with customers had a low inner level of motivation and as a result of this, not surprisingly, their commercial results were lower than those of their better motivated colleagues. Prolonged low-level motivation makes results harder to achieve: it limits what you can actually attain.

## So How Do You Get Motivated?

First, I want to say that this is down to you – no one else can do this for you, although there are those who can inspire and encourage you (think about those "Radiators").

So here are my 5 top tips on Self Motivation:

1. Install a healthy, empowering self-belief system. I will show you how to do this as you work your way through the *You Selling You Programme*.

2. Master your inner dialogue and when you are aware that you are talking yourself down, I want you to visualise a large sign with the word STOP! written on it and I want you to hear the word shouted out loud.

3. Identify something or someone that can instantly trigger a more positive, motivated you. In my own case, thinking about my niece

helps; often thinking about our children and those dear to us can do the trick. Or maybe the thought of a beloved pet works for us. Focusing on our beliefs, maybe our Church community helps e.g. the more successful we are materially, the more we can donate to charity. Maybe the idea of material wealth, a holiday, a new car etc can be the trigger to get us going.

4. Reward your achievements. One business manager told me that his reward for exceeding his commercial targets would be to take his family to Euro Disney for a week. In a way he used this as his trigger to succeed. Focusing on this, he exceeded his target by 12% in what was a competitive market. Rewards needn't be so big though: quality time for yourself or a bunch of flowers or new outfit still say "Well done."

5. Take in a piece of action each day. For example, if your goal is to get fit, then each day do something that contributes to that e.g. 45 sit-ups on Monday; 60 press-ups on Tuesday etc. Each of these small actions will contribute collectively to overall success.

If you are aware that your motivation is very, very low; that you are at rock bottom and constantly feel dull and sluggish, try getting up and moving around; get your heart pumping and your blood circulating. You'd be surprised how something as simple as going for a short walk can re-energise you.

One way to help get started is to record your actions and your progress. You've already begun by writing down your answers to the five questions on page 21. But, just to make a clearer commitment to yourself, maybe you could make a compact such as the one on the next page:

---

**You Selling You Promise:**

I ............................................. (name)  deserve to reach my full potential.

I will spend time developing my skills and talents in order to achieve my goals.

I will work through each of the sections of the *You Selling You Programme*.


Signed: ............................................... Date: ........................

---

# 1. The Ground Rules and Understanding the Concept.

So now you've put it in writing, put it into action. Here you will be given a summary of the interrelated steps you will work through in *You Selling You*. This programme includes a number of exercises that will increase your mental strength. It has become part of life to go to the gym on a weekly or even a daily basis. I want to make it your goal to combine this physical exercise with a mental workout.

## The Ground Rules of *You Selling You.*

Let's begin by taking a look at fundamental ground rules: the corner pieces of the jigsaw. Take note of all of the ground rules noting clearly what each will mean for you.

\#   Read no further unless your heart is in this process to make the most of YOU.

\#   Take responsibility and avoid blame - before I found the secret to success I put my energy into blaming other people when things didn't work out for me or I felt I deserved better than I was getting. I thought "they" could provide me with a road map to enter the world of winners.

**It wasn't until I took the "b" out of blame that I realised what I was.**

\#   Get excited. Be turned on by the idea of your success. Let the thought of it wash through you and fill you with desire.

\#   Be prepared to take action each day to implement the *You Selling You Programme*. Make it happen. Don't wait for it to happen. Action is at the heart of my message here. *You Selling You* requires you to take steps forward, to journey on the road ahead without constantly looking back. Are you prepared for that?

\#   Be prepared to step out of your comfort zone. Some of the actions I recommend that you take will require both effort and courage. Along the way, you need to have a flexible approach and to enjoy the process as you take creative steps forward.

> *Only those who dare to fail greatly can ever achieve greatly:* John F Kennedy

\#   Become open minded: how many times have you heard it said that the map is not the territory. Isn't it about time you started stepping outside the territory?

And remember, it is important that all 6 ground rules are adhered to, if you are to make the difference you're after. Understanding the concept is crucial and as you progress with the programme, you will see how all the pieces of the process work together to create the picture of a successful you.

## 2. Dissociating Old Habits.

How many times have you been at a meeting when there has been something you really want to say, but something stops you? Or you may recall being at an interview: you know you're right for the job and have a lot to offer, but something stops you from presenting yourself in the best light: you stop short of selling yourself.

I remember working with a young professional, who was actually doing especially well in her career. What she wanted from me was help in increasing her confidence in her personal life so that she could more easily form new relationships. Work was safe and comfortable and whenever necessary she could put forward her most positive and engaging persona. However, when it came to forming close personal relationships, she found this more difficult. For years she had told herself that she was not particularly attractive – she had established a negative inner dialogue. This repeated belief about herself was blocking her ability to build relationships, other than professional ones. It had led to behavioural habits that were unhelpful.

We have all experienced times like these. Times when the only thing that is stopping us from taking the action we want, or from putting ourselves forward for what we want, is something inside ourselves. It isn't others who are stopping our progress; it's not "them"; it's us.

We can view the things that stop us from developing as emotional blockages and these blockages need to be flushed away - a bit like unblocking a sink.

I remember talking to John, a 40 year old Senior Manager. He could always plan a most sophisticated presentation, but when it came to delivering the said presentation, he couldn't do it very well. He could never make the most of his knowledge and his preparation. Something blocked him. During a session with him, I noted that he repeated the following idea at least 12 times:

**"there's just something that stops me."**

It was clear we had to find out what this "something" was. As we explored his issue, it became apparent that what stopped John from performing was related to anxieties – anxieties that had been reinforced over years through replication of a particular internal state. Accumulated anxieties were blocking John's progress. What John needed was to clear this blockage, flush out the debris of anxiety that had built up over time.

Maxwell Maltz explains in his book *Psycho Cybernetics* – every so often we need an Emotional Makeover. This is what John needed; it is what we all need now and again.

One of the activities you will undertake in the *You Selling You Programme* will be to identify your debilitating blockages, regardless of where they have come from and how you have allowed them to build up. You will pinpoint them and then remove them, leaving yourself open for positive and helpful thoughts and emotions. This action will ensure that you are free to release your true potential.

## 3. Affirming You Can.

As you may be aware, organisations spend millions each year on marketing and not without good cause. There is ample academic research and hard evidence to demonstrate that marketing really does work. On a course I was delivering, I once asked this simple question: "What is marketing as part of the process of business?" Lisa a 29 year old advertising executive was the first to answer.

She said: *it was the process of creating desire in people.*

I then discussed with the group HOW marketing created that desire. I came to the conclusion that marketing is simply the power of **REPEATED SUGGESTION** and that this conditioned the thought processes of the consumer by increasing their desire to purchase a particular product or service.

Bearing this in mind, the great news is that you can utilise this principle for *You Selling You*. In other words, you can repeat and reinforce ideas internally that will help you in the marketing of yourself. Repeating suggestions or affirmations, will build up positive and empowering thoughts and emotions about you. This internal work will be an important foundation to the *You Selling You Programme.*

**YOUR INTERNAL AFFIRMATION WILL DETERMINE THE QUALITY OF YOUR EXTERNAL SUGGESTION TO OTHERS.**

We've all had our successes, though, and maybe you can think back to a time when you really knew you could do something and you followed through and did it. Maybe there has been a time when you felt deep inside you that things would work out for you and lo and behold, they did.

You may have thought that this was lucky chance or coincidence and that fortune was smiling on you at that time.

ACTUALLY your own positive beliefs played a major role in your success.

## 4.  Installing Belief in your Brilliance/Putting Your Winning Stake Together.

Later in the book, when you read about the **how** of *You Selling You*, you will receive advice on dissociating blockages. You can liken this process to emptying the trash. Think about it, when you empty the trash can, it's only a matter of hours before you have filled it back up with similar garbage. In *You Selling You*, you will be dissociating your particular garbage, i.e. getting rid of it, but then you will be shown how to fill yourself back up with individual brilliance, rather than allow the same old rubbish to return.

Belief is the key to this and the knowledge that you have a choice. You can either decide to continue to fill yourself up with limiting beliefs that keep you static, or decide to install empowering beliefs that move you on into the world of winners.

During your work on this part of the programme, I will not be suggesting that you simply stand in front of the mirror telling yourself how wonderful you are (although please feel free to do so) but I will be explaining how you can use a psycho-physiological process that can be embedded deep into your way of being and which will become part of your everyday conditioning.

Let's think about how the idea of belief fits into our lives. There is no doubt that belief is the seed of the confidence that will grow into action and achievement. Belief determines your perception, which in turn determines your actions and the quality of your actions and the ensuing results. Ultimately these results lead to a final outcome, which in turn reinforces belief: and so the perpetual cycle of positive affirmation begins.

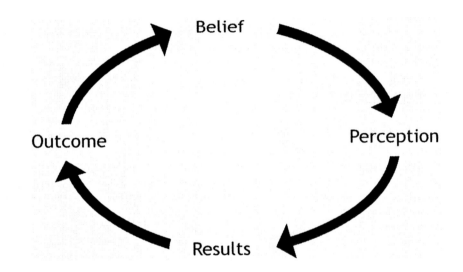

## 5. Communication Excellence.

Once your Internal State is developed, you will begin to find the quality and results of your external communications begin to be more effective. External Communication combines both verbal and non-verbal cues, including that which is your personal image. It is my view that it would be a fool, who in this day and age, considers that image plays no part in determining both personal and business achievement. It may be the reasonable thing to say, "it's what's on the inside that counts," but in reality the outside is equally important and it's our outside that we are first judged by.

I have spoken to a number of style and image specialists during the course of writing this book and their accounts will show why our physical image requires attention and development. They also show where a positive change in personal image has added value to those wanting to sell themselves and achieve their goals.

## 6. Lifting Your Personal Profile and Inspiring Others.

You are your own success story.

Have you ever wondered why successful people achieve and continue to achieve? It has been my opinion for many years that they "play the movie" of their success and power in their mind, to such a degree, that it becomes an automatic conditioning. Their "movie" is planned, written and shot with success in mind. As you read on, you will be challenged to write and play your own movie of success; to identify the key actions, the words, the moves etc that you will need to take, actions which will become major players in *You Selling You*.

Take William, a newly appointed Senior Manager, whose challenge was to lead change in his organisation. He was running a large sales team, half of whom were unfocused, negative and turning in poor results. William could not let this situation continue and needed to take action for change. I was called to meet with him to provide business coaching to support his personal effectiveness in driving that change forward. As well as support for the design of his business strategy, it became apparent that he needed help in boosting his personal presence. My diagnosis here was that he needed to anchor the image of his success story into his mind, aligned with an empowering belief, so that he could execute the selling of himself to win the hearts and minds of his people; they had to believe in him before they could buy into his business strategy, and the only way they would do that was if he believed in himself.

To achieve satisfaction in a demanding world, lifting your personal profile is more important than ever before, with applications relevant to, amongst other things, leadership, career development, sales and customer service.

You may already be starting to think clearly about the things you want to believe of yourself and how this can help you to create your own success: that's good.

**You may also be starting to visualise your own movie of success.**

Once your internal self is looked after, groomed and nurtured, it is at this point that you are ready and probably more willing to step out of your comfort zone and take your first practical steps.

---

Think back to David, the 23 year old Senior Sales Executive. When he used to visit his clients, he would arrive at his destination, but then sit in the car park and endure a flood of anxiety. The more he allowed this to happen, the worse he felt. He let himself believe that he couldn't do the job he'd come to do, that he'd be no good. There were many occasions when he would simply take the escape route and call and cancel the meeting with the client. It was impossible at this time for him to impress his abilities on others. He wasn't ready to take the important steps that would take him on a new road to success. Following steps 1 – 6 of the *You Selling You Programme*, began to prepare him to change his dismal situation.

---

Impressing ourselves upon others is the next natural step to *You Selling You*.

Having sorted your internal self, it is at that point I am certain you will begin to notice that you automatically begin to make changes in practical ways to sell yourself; that you really want to make those changes. As well as **thinking** about actions you want to do as a result of your internal state, *You Selling You* is about turning the starting key, which will allow you to take that first step that will turn thought into **action** to produce a new reality.

## Let's Turn That Key ...

I want you to begin thinking about what your first step will be. What is the first scene in your movie? What is the location? Write the script:

E.g. 1: maybe you want to sell yourself to gain promotion. You believe it's right for you. You tell yourself: "I believe I can do it. I feel positive and confident. I've installed positive beliefs. I can visualise success happening."

E.g. 2: maybe you seek to increase your role as a business development professional. You begin to tell yourself that it is possible and that it is you, as a personality, who can influence your prospects. Maybe you begin to see the result as a possibility, right now. See yourself having sold you and consequently, your product and or service.

E.g. 3: maybe you are an actor, performer, teacher or presenter. You are telling yourself, "I am focused and confident." You notice the delight of your audience, their engagement with you and their desire for more of you. You see yourself acknowledging and congratulating your success.

E.g. 4: perhaps you want to portray yourself in the best light to new people. Maybe you want to strike a new relationship and decide you want to get in shape. You say to yourself, "I am a successful slimmer." And deep in your mind you maintain this energy and focus by saying to yourself, "I am confident and vibrant; I communicate with ease."

## So What Now?

Somehow you need to influence those who can help you achieve the results you desire. Part of the *You Selling You* process will involve thinking clearly about other players in our movie: the recipients of our "sales pitch" and how we will inspire them to "buy".

## Networking.

Others can influence your success in *You Selling You.*

During the process, you may at times want to share what you are doing with others. Beware! There are those who have a negative approach to life, those who will seek to plant a seed of doubt in your mind about the validity of this work and even about your right to succeed. People may suggest that they don't want you to change or that by focusing on your own progress that you are being selfish. They may not say this directly but you know the implication is there. Be aware that this may happen and don't be swayed by it. What other people mean when they try to divert you from developing is that they are scared that you will leave them behind, that they may be envious of your success, that they want your attention for themselves; they are worried that you will not meet their needs - think about it. Who's the selfish one? Other folks may undermine what you do by dismissing what you say as psychobabble. So what? You know the reality of this programme; you are the one experiencing it, reaping its benefits, so who cares what others call it.

Fortunately, however, there are also those people who are positive and supportive. As you yourself become more this way inclined, you will be more alert to the benefit of having such individuals around. Associate with these people that feed you, encourage you and inspire you.

Think now of whom the players will be in your movie; that will help you achieve your goals.

Maybe you will need to make connections with some of your customers, who will then influence other customers and this may lead to an increase in your sales figures. Maybe other professionals can help facilitate your career progression. Perhaps there is the prospect of meeting new people who can support your career or relationship goals.

Help make it happen for you, **by surrounding yourself with people who radiate positive energy, and stay away from those who drain your energy and focus.**

## NOW...

TAKE THE ACTION that will help actualise your desires. This can be the point of make or break, winning or losing. It can determine whether you will be a finisher or a non-starter.

We will look closely now at the process that will help you to your success: the **how** of the programme.

**But before you continue, just reflect on whether *You Selling You* is for you:**

# APPLICATIONS OF *YOU SELLING YOU*

*You Selling You* is for anyone who wants to develop greater influence over others.

It is written for an eclectic audience and the concept may be applied to a wide variety of situations including:

- Leaders, in all sectors, wanting to inspire those for whom they are responsible.
- Directors and managers at all levels.
- Business Development specialists determined to influence their clients to sign business contracts.
- Presenters, actors, teachers whose personal performance has an impact upon their "audience".
- Senior professionals who want to ensure they gain a high level personal profile within their organisation.
- Individuals searching for a career change or a new role and who want to impress at interviews.
- Those wanting to develop effective relationships with others, including customers, colleagues and other stakeholders who can have an influence on their personal results and progress.
- Human Resource and Training professionals wanting to influence in powerful ways within their organisation through their own behaviours as well as building the ideas from *You Selling You* concept into training and development programmes.
- Sales professionals who want to ensure their behaviours influence existing clients and prospects to ultimately "close the deal."
- An individual who wants to boost their impact on other people to achieve both personal and professional objectives.

# PART 1:

## INNER WORK

**Step 1**
**The Ground Rules and**
**Understanding the Concept**

**Step 2**
**Dissociating Old Habits**

**Step 3**
**Affirming You Can**

**Step 4**
**Installing Belief in your**
**Brilliance**

## STEP 1: THE GROUND RULES AND UNDERSTANDING THE CONCEPT

As you read, you will be given a number of techniques to increase and support the power of your mind. Why? Well your ability to use your mind to its full potential will enable you to best create an inner state that is conducive to success and it is your internal self that will ultimately determine the quality of *You Selling You*. Before we get to the active part of the programme, it may be as well to understand what it is we're working with.

### The Mind.

Your mind is split into two parts, namely the *conscious* and the *unconscious.* Let's take a look at what this means.

a) **the conscious mind** – this is represented by your current awareness, your thoughts, feelings and current here and now experiences.

b) **the unconscious mind** – this is represented by your memories and experiences that have been "forgotten". In other words these memories and experiences are out of your conscious awareness, although they may well become conscious again under the right circumstances. For example, you may have had a negative experience when selling a product to a client – maybe the client became awkward, or asked you questions you couldn't answer. Although that uncomfortable experience is done and dusted, in the past and consigned to your unconscious mind, you may find yourself in circumstances which are similar enough to trigger the negative emotions you previously felt. The experience and its associated feelings, which lay dormant in your unconscious, are once again made conscious. This in turn may affect your effectiveness in your current situation.

It is also within the unconscious that individuals carry their defence mechanisms: defence mechanisms which are there to protect you from unnecessary emotional pain. These same safeguards may, however, hold you back from executing the healthy behaviours you need to put into practice for *You Selling You*. Some typical defence mechanisms include:-

i)   Denial – avoiding certain situations that we think will feel uncomfortable e.g. avoiding delivering business presentations or if you work in sales, avoiding an opportunity to make cold calls.

ii)  Displacement – transferring emotional feelings from their original cause or object to one that disguises their real nature. This may involve blaming other people rather than taking personal responsibility.

iii) Deflection – changing the subject to avoid a perceived uncomfortable event e.g. changing the conversation quickly.

iv)  Compensation – an over-the-top expression of "being the best" when in fact the real you feels vulnerable and insecure. Here a person tries to conceal their weaknesses and shortcomings by an exaggerated exhibition of other qualities e.g. a man may act over tough to hide his softer more feminine side.

v)   Reaction formation – a way of protecting the self against some repressed wish. This is when someone condemns something on a conscious level, which deep down, on the unconscious level, they desire.

The creative techniques that follow will support you in tapping the power of your mind. They are designed to strengthen your mental processes so you gradually become comfortable to show the world your confidence and your natural vibrant persona. The inner work that you undertake, will help to naturally melt your defences so that you can begin to sell yourself effectively and with ease to a more appropriate level, in a wide variety of situations.

Notice I use the words **naturally** and **with ease**. There really is a difference between natural confidence and a forced confidence, which isn't really confidence at all. My processes will help you exhibit a natural, genuine confidence so that *You Selling You* becomes part of your being – in other words part and parcel of your unconscious process.

## **Individual States of Awareness.**

Human beings are operating at their optimum when they are holding 7 pieces of information in their short-term memory at any one time. Bearing this in mind, I want to explain to you something called the **7 +/- 2 model**.

When we hold 7 pieces of information, as said, that is our norm. When we hold 8 pieces of information we are operating with an overly busy mind, which is often termed **neurotic**. Being in this state can be fine for a period of time and as long as when the extra unit of information is no longer required we return readily and easily to our normal 7 piece functioning. But what happens if we go from 7 to 8 to 9? What occurs when we hold 2 pieces of information above our norm? Well this is when we would be diagnosed as having a **psychosis**! The good news is this is rare.

Now let's look at the reverse problem. What happens when we hold only 6 pieces of information in our short-term memory? This is when we would become **lethargic,** which although not ideal, is still safe and healthy. But when we drop to only holding 5 pieces, then our state would be described as **catatonic** – definitely not the norm or healthy.

Fortunately, the vast majority of us carry 6 – 8 pieces of information around in our short-term memory at any one time. The *You Selling You* programme holds helpful suggestions for you when you're burdened with 8 pieces of information (7+1) which leads to neurotic behaviour. These suggestions will help you create a sense of calm and a feeling of being at ease. There are also helpful ideas for when you are lethargic – when you have only 6 pieces of information (7-1). These will help motivate, inspire and energise you. It is when you have this sense of balance, between neuroticism and lethargy that you will be in a psychological state that helps you exert the potential to sell yourself.

> **HOW...**
> ...do you implement the *You Selling You Programme*?

If you are still reading, my guess is that you have made a commitment to yourself – the commitment to follow the *You Selling You Programme* – the commitment to discover your excellence and share it with the world. I will help you with this by taking you through a process, which will enable you to reap the rewards of the *You Selling You* formula.

As you follow my recommendations, please keep an open mind. Much of what I will guide you through will involve your cognitive processes and will ask you to question the way you think. You will be examining what goes on in your mind and you will be feeding your internal state with new and maybe unfamiliar fare. As a result, some exercises may at first appear strange. They may also be a challenge, as you will be focusing on thinking which is deep rooted and which may not be easy to shift or alter. I ask you to trust me and stick with the programme. I assure you, it will be well worth the effort. I have seen the processes I describe in this book, work time and time again for many people from all walks of life. I want you to share in this and find out for yourself just how effective you can be.

My commitment to you is to guide you on a journey that I have witnessed working for many people; a journey I have no doubt will lead you to a better place. Your commitment is to give your heart and mind to it.

During your work you will need to carry with you those ground rules we covered earlier; take them with you as you work through the steps in the programme. It may be a good idea to remind yourself of these rules right now.

Broadly speaking, the *You Selling You Programme* can be divided into two main areas: the **Internal** work and **External** work. Your first job is to deal with your Internal State. This will prepare you for work on your External State when you will focus on recommended practical activities and exercises. On the *You Selling You Programme*, it is important to start with attention to the Internal State, before embarking on the External State, but as we progress, you will see how interdependent the two states are.

## The Iceberg.

Think of an Iceberg. What we see above the surface of the water is only a portion of the whole. The bulk of the berg is beneath the surface, hidden and unseen. We can liken ourselves to this. What others see of us, on the surface, is only part of our makeup; the bulk of who we are lies below and unseen. But it is this part of us, the part which lies beneath, that determines the quality of the part of us that others see. In other words, our inner makeup determines our outer demeanour.

personal projection;
skills; behaviour

— — — — — — — — — — — — — — —

beliefs; emotions; thoughts; feelings
imagination; inner dialogue
self-esteem

I can't underestimate the importance of this so let me give you another example – the actor. When an actor prepares for a role, in order to give a truthful and believable interpretation of his character, he will pay attention to the inner life of the character he is creating as well as the character's outer appearance. In the rehearsal period, it is the inner preparation of a role i.e. finding the emotional truth and creating the imaginative world of the role that helps lead to a convincing external performance; it helps the actor to sell the role to his audience. You may be wondering what this has to do with your development – you aren't an actor acting a role, you are being you. But you can learn from it. You play out the role of who you are on a daily basis. Ask yourself this question. Are you giving the best performance of who you are and is it a performance of who you want to be?

## Record Your Progress and Maintain the Ground Rules.

Before you read on, I want you to go and find a notebook. You will use this as a diary and in your diary you will keep a record of the steps you take each day. Make it a part of your daily routine to note what you have done to contribute to *You Selling You.*

Why is this important? Well, the diary will help ensure you maintain your focus. It will provide concrete evidence of your progress and show that you are moving forward. You will see your triumphs recorded and this in turn will boost your self-esteem. In fact one of the key aspects of this journey is the "revving up" of your self-esteem.

What do I mean by that? I mean that you'll begin to have a proper estimation of your own worth and people who have "proper worth" are good to have around, achieve more naturally and sell themselves to others in an effortless way. And where does self-esteem start? It starts on the inside, in our minds. So let's begin the process of internal work, but before you do, just remind yourself that YOU DESERVE THIS.

Start your diary right away: it would be a good idea to write out the Ground Rules on page 1 and then we can start on our workout of your Internal State.

Also make certain you continue to comply with the Ground Rules of the *You Selling You Programme*. Doing so will make certain you begin to make progress.

## **The Internal State.**

There are 3 processes you will be taking as we work on your Internal State:

Dissociating Old Habits
Affirmation
Playing the story of your success

## STEP 2: DISSOCIATING OLD HABITS

Learning to relax deeply has to be your first step. Why? Because resting the conscious part of your mind will enable you to access the unconscious hidden part of you. As I explained, basically what you have to do is to work with those parts of you that are deep within i.e. the unconscious. You need to groom and enhance these elements to empower the parts of you that the world sees e.g. your personal projection and behaviours.

For years and years I have no doubt that many of you who read this book will have programmed your mind with "demon garbage" over and over again. Replication of this has meant that you may have conditioned yourself with a store of limiting barriers that have blocked your ability to sell you. In order to change, you will need to reprogramme your mind. You will need to get rid of the debilitating rubbish that has hindered your progress and replace it with something more nurturing and encouraging. To do this necessary internal work, your conscious mind needs to rest so that you can work deeply within your unconscious process. The only way to do this is through relaxation.

Let's just think of our actor again. A significant aspect of actor training is relaxation. This is not only so that the actor moves freely, naturally and safely, but also so that he can access his inner world more easily: his thought processes, his emotional life and his imagination. When Constantin Stanislavski, the father of modern actor training, devised his system to help actors develop their skills and creativity, he demonstrated how failure to relax impedes the inner processes. In one exercise, he asked his students to try and lift a heavy piano. One by one the students attempted to do so, lifting one corner of the object off the ground. Whilst they held up the heavy instrument, Stanislavski asked his students to quickly multiply 37 x 9 – but they couldn't do it. He asked them to use their memories to recall all the shops along the street that the theatre was on. Again they couldn't do it. He gave them other tests: to sing a familiar song, to remember the taste of kidney stew, the feel of silk, the smell of something burning. In order to respond easily to the questions, students found they needed to relax their muscles and put down the heavy piano. Whilst tense they struggled to access their inner experiences. Tension did not just impede the actors physically, but also spiritually as well. Doesn't this show all the more reason to induce a state of relaxation when attempting to work on the Internal State?

And the Iceberg? Imagine it. An iceberg is frozen, rigid, and solid. We need to "melt" it a little to start to shift and begin to change some of our hidden beliefs and perceptions. We can do this through relaxation.

Before I give you guidance on how to achieve a state of relaxation, let me explain the theory to the process, so that you engage in the experience with understanding of what you are doing. If you have knowledge about the processes you undertake, it allows you to take on responsibility for what you do.

## Brainwaves: Where Relaxation Fits.

Your brain transmits 4 different kinds of brainwave, each resulting in a different state within you. By appreciating the characteristics of each type of brainwave, you will be in a position to take advantage of that knowledge to accelerate rapid change from within.

### Alpha State.
During the alpha state, there are 8 – 12 brainwave cycles per second. The alpha state is also known as "Relaxed Alertness". Let me give you an example of this. Driving to a destination have you ever, upon arrival, realised that you cannot remember anything about the journey you took?

Or maybe you have been curled up on the sofa with a book, warm and comfy in front of the fire – someone has called your name, but whilst the sounds of that call have entered your ears, your conscious brain hasn't registered it. In both examples, your mind has rested to the point when although not asleep, it isn't totally alert to its surroundings.

This state is accompanied by feelings of inner calm and rest. This is the state you will enter when you practise your relaxation exercises. It is a state that enables unconscious reprogramming – it is the state that needs to be accessed to begin your inner work. Your alpha state will help you access a wealth of creativity that lies just below your conscious awareness.

## Beta State
During your beta state, you are fully awake. This state is often referred to as "Full Conscious Alertness". During the beta state, there are 13+ brainwave cycles per second. When you are in the beta state, relaxation cannot be deep and unconscious reprogramming is therefore more difficult as the conscious mind is too busy. This state is associated with full concentration and heightened alertness.

## Theta State
During the theta state you will have 4 – 7 brainwave cycles per second. This state is often referred to as the early stages of sleep. In this state, you have moved from the Alpha State and are drifting down to a deeper level. During years of explaining the different brainwave states to my clients, many have commented that in the theta state, their body experiences sudden movement e.g. whilst drifting off to sleep, they have suddenly jerked awake. During the theta state, you enjoy the first stages of sleep and you're mind begins to process information from the day.

You may ask why then the theta state isn't the best for our purposes – well the reason is that it is important to be awake enough to do the reprogramming required. In the theta state, this is not the case.

## Delta State

During the delta state, there are ½ - 3 brainwave cycles per second. This is when you are deeply asleep and unconscious.

BRAINWAVE STATES

|  | ALPHA | BETA | THETA | DELTA |
|---|---|---|---|---|
| Cycles per second | 8 - 12 | 13+ | 4 - 7 | ½ -3 |
| Description | Relaxed Alertness | Full Conscious Alertness | Early Stages of Sleep | Deep Sleep |

## It's easier said than done, so how do you relax?

On the next page, I guide you through 10 steps that will help you to induce relaxation in yourself. You may not find it easy to begin with, but like with any skill, you will get better and more accomplished with practise. Believe me; you will not regret acquiring the ability to Induce Personal Relaxation. Why? Because this is an essential part of the process that will enable re-programming to take place. I advise you to read through the 10 steps first and make sure that you understand what is involved in the process and what to expect. Once you have familiarised yourself with the 10 steps –

## HAVE A GO!

But first a caution. For obvious reasons, do not attempt the following whilst driving or operating machinery, or where relaxing too deeply may affect your personal safety.

## Step 1

Find a comfortable, warm place. The reason for this is that your body temperature will drop as you relax. Make sure it's somewhere you will not be disturbed. This obviously also means putting the answer phone on and turning off the mobile.

## Step 2
Sit upright in a comfortable chair. I always recommend to my clients that they do not lie down. As human beings, when we lie down, we are conditioned to fall asleep. Allow the chair to support your body and sink into it comfortably.

## Step 3
Place your feet flat on the floor, with your hands resting on your thighs and allow your eyes to gently close. It is quite normal for thoughts to be drifting through your mind. Avoid fighting them. In fact you may allow your mind to focus even more on those thoughts that you consider distract you.

## Step 4
Allow any external noises to drift in and out of your mind e.g. traffic, people in the distance, aircraft, a clock ticking. The secret here is to blend these external noises into your relaxation process e.g. you may internally suggest to yourself that each tick of the clock helps you drift a little deeper into the relaxed state or as each car passes, you "melt" into a deeper state of relaxation.

## Step 5
Imagine a peaceful scene – it maybe a place that you know, that you have visited or maybe it is somewhere you have imagined or dreamt about. Focus on your breathing as you conjure up your scene. Notice what you see and what you hear. Begin to notice the feelings that accompany your scene.

## Step 6
Slowly start to work down the muscles of your body – I emphasise the word SLOWLY. The mind needs time. With each group of muscles, imagine them becoming a little tired, a little floppy or maybe a little heavier. Begin with the muscles of the face including the cheeks, lips and jaw.

Gradually move your attention to the shoulders, arms and fingers. Slowly move to the chest, stomach and back. Ultimately continue through to the thighs, calves and feet. Remember that this process must be carried out slowly. Allow yourself time to enjoy this warm, comforting sense of complete calm. Allow time for the feeling to penetrate your depths.

## Step 7

Now, again slowly, count down from 10 – 1. Tell yourself that with each number you will drift a little more deeply into the wonderful state of relaxation and calm. Ensure you count each number on every other out breath. In your mind you can also imagine you are becoming deeper and deeper relaxed, more and more drowsy. This step will help deepen further your relaxation. Again carry out this process slowly, perhaps in your mind noticing how you drift deeper and deeper into this state of calm.

## Step 8

Once your countdown has been completed, select one word, e.g. "calm", "ease" or simply "relaxed". Tell yourself that in a few moments you will hear yourself say your chosen word 6 times and that each time you say the word you will become twice as deeply relaxed. Tell yourself that as you say the word any tension will float out through your fingers and toes. Repeat your word on every other out breath. For example…..*"and now…I am deeply relaxed…and in a few moments I will hear myself say the word…calm…and as I repeat the word….calm…any remaining tension will drift out through my fingers…and out through my toes….so…calm…"*

## Step 9

Following this one word "installation" allow yourself to enjoy the depth of relaxation that you have reached for about 5 minutes. You may find it helps during this time to occasionally repeat your cue word.

## Step 10

Having enjoyed the process of relaxing, it is important to fully awaken yourself. To do this tell yourself that in a few moments you will count up from 1 – 10 and at the count of 7 you will open your eyes and at the count of 10 you will be completely back in the room and any feelings of heaviness will have disappeared. You can also suggest to yourself that you will awaken feeling calm, confident, alert and fully wide awake. So now, count up from 1 – 10. Tell yourself that every part of you will be back in the room.

Over the years, this has always been the first technique I have taught my clients. It is the equivalent of turning the ignition key of the *You Selling You Programme*.

Over the next 3 days simply practise the relaxation protocol as described. At first it may feel awkward and difficult, but like everything, familiarity and practise will help make it second nature.

Do not read on until you feel you have comfortably not only understood the protocol of self induced relaxation, but you can apply it too.

## ENJOY.

Mastering Step 2 is significant to the progress of *You Selling You*.

Just before we move on though, a further word regarding Relaxation. In the *You Selling You Programme*, we use it first of all to ensure our minds are in the optimum state to affect internal change. There are, however other benefits. Relaxation helps us rid ourselves of unnecessary physical tension. This in turn helps us to use our bodies and voices in a much more effective manner. Tension in the diaphragm interferes with our breathing and our voice can become thin and lack power. Muscle tension can make our movements unnatural, our facial expressions strained. If we are to play our roles to best effect, tension is the last thing we need.

You will see quite clearly these benefits of Relaxation when we work on the External State. You will be rewarded with the freedom to act with vibrancy and make clear personal impact – to ensure that you are remembered and stand out from the crowd. Think back to any times when communication between yourself and another has been blocked – this is likely to have been because you or the other person was carrying excess tension. This excess tension communicates itself on an unconscious level and leads to uncomfortable and non-productive dialogue.

When working with Field Sales Professionals I spend much time training and coaching them in making their dialogue with clients comfortable and effective – naturally if this is not the case, then results and relationships suffer. The first thing I get my clients to do is to learn to relax their body and their mind, so that they are in a state to really engage their clients and motivate their desire for their product or service. Until they are able to do this, then other ideas I suggest will not have maximum impact.

It is true that an individual will not sell themselves when they are engaged in a stress response. Anxiety triggers a fight/flight response when your body prepares to protect itself from harm. Take for instance the times you have been faced with a challenge from a customer or tough questions at an interview and you have found your physiological and mental state become filled with symptoms of hyper anxiety. The instinctive reaction is to either fight back which may mean you become aggressive or submit completely.

The good news is that we can prepare our minds to take on such challenges and react to them in a much more appropriate manner. You can by learning to be more relaxed to such events pump up your mind with confidence to handle them appropriately, professionally and effectively.

By practicing relaxation you will support your autonomic nervous system in maintaining equilibrium. The autonomic nervous system has two main components, the sympathetic nervous system which is responsible for action and the parasympathetic nervous system which is responsible for rest.

As a healthy individual you will have both components in balance. When faced with a challenging situation the sympathetic nervous system is active and action is taken. Once the challenging situation has passed the parasympathetic nervous system will take over and calm your body down and help equilibrium to take place. For those who do not practice relaxation in some form the sympathetic nervous system response is predominantly active and may result in poor results, low level motivation and in some cases poor health.

---

### Check Your Progress:

1. Why is it essential to learn to induce a state of relaxation when working on creating the internal state to support *You Selling You?*

2. Think of a few key words that you will say to yourself as you teach yourself to relax, which you can use to help you induce a state of deep relaxation: note them in your diary.

3. Make a note of where and when you will practise relaxation over the next 3 days.

4. Remind yourself of the key stages in engaging relaxation until this becomes second nature.

5. How will you reward yourself for your disciplined approach to learning relaxation?

---

## Using Your New Skill.

Having learnt how to install a state of relaxation, you can use your new skill to help dissociate old negative habits.

How many times have you been in a situation where you've said to yourself, "I want to do this, but there's part of me that just won't let me." Or maybe you've had the feeling that something blocks you from doing the very thing that in your heart you want to do. I believe that on an unconscious level, we tend to create for ourselves an internal "mess" that over time accumulates and coagulates to form blockages that slow us down. You could liken this to speed bumps in the road; those frustrating ramps that make us drop a gear and impede our progress. In the case of our internal ramps, however, they just get bigger and bigger until we are unable to make any progress at all. We find we have developed unhelpful patterns of behaviour, either through repeated, disempowering internal dialogue or through experiences where things have gone wrong on so many occasions.

Some people may think that some form of therapy may help to identify our emotional blocks and discover what caused them. This is fine, but what do you do with this information? Continually talking about the past can sometimes keep us in the past. Knowing why we are the way we are is one of the steps to self-awareness, but can this change anything? What comes next? How do we unhook from what holds us back?

I will help you begin to shift these blockages and to change the negative to positive. The exercises that I provide you with rely on your ability to use your imaginative capacities. So before we go further with the *You Selling You Programme*, let us just take a few moments to use this force within you. Note that I use the word "force". Imagination is a very powerful tool.

Think of our actor again. He needs to exercise his imagination in order to create a role and if an actor's imagination is not very strong, he takes the trouble to develop it. Similarly, imagination can play an enormous part in the creation of your new reality and if you feel that you are lacking in this area, you too can improve simply by exercising this faculty.

So let's have a go and use your imagination:
Close your eyes and imagine that:
- you have just bitten into a slice of lemon
- you are breathing in the scent of a rose
- you are running your hand over a piece of velvet
- you are standing in and looking at your bedroom
- you are sitting across from a close friend and see their face
- you listen to the voice of that friend
- you place your hand on the trunk of a tree
- you are enjoying your favourite food

How was this exercise for you? Were you able to do this easily? Were some things easier to imagine than others? Maybe some of you found it easy to imagine something you were visualising, whereas others of you found it easier to imagine sounds, tastes, smells or the touch of things.

Many of you will see, from this simple exercise, just how powerful the imagination is. Think of the first task, for example. Most people find that they wince at the bitterness of the lemon taste and that they salivate, even though there is no actual lemon producing this reaction. The reactions are created solely by the mind. That is because your mind does not know what is real and what is not.

The above exercises ask you to recreate in your mind familiar experiences, but imagination can also be used to create those things, which are as yet unfamiliar. Maybe you have never given a business presentation with confidence, but there's nothing to stop you imagining yourself doing that very thing.

When you undertake the following dissociation exercises and create through your imagination, do so in as much detail as you can. As Stanislavski told his actors: *you must not think it out "somehow" or "in general" or "approximately".*

As you develop your skill, move from being passive to active in imagination: to be a spectator of the imaginary life is passive; to picture yourself in the imaginary life is also passive; to no longer see yourself, but to see and experience through the senses what surrounds you in the imaginary life is active.

Soon, you will find that your unconscious mind will respond to your conscious efforts and will begin to further facilitate any necessary transition. It will take away the "parts" or blockages responsible for unwanted behaviour and replace them with more resourceful "parts" that will enable you to effectively sell you.

In order to dissociate your blockages you will need to utilise your new founded ability to relax. What you'll be doing is carrying out an emotional clearance in your mind so you can reprogramme your unconscious state. In simple terms, you'll be clearing your mind of the "mess" but not refilling it with the same old rubbish.

---

Guy is a 25 year old law graduate who visited me with an interview phobia. He had a first class honours degree and one would have imagined that his achievements would have carried him all the way to wherever he wanted to go, but no, they didn't. Guy was anxious that, because of his fears, he would never secure the job he knew deep down he could do. There was nothing wrong with Guy's ambitions; he wanted to work for and with the best and he had sent his CV to a number of excellent law firms. His worry was that he would stumble at the next hurdle – the interview.

Having coached Guy to relax to a deep level, it was important for him to draw out **the part** that was responsible for creating his hyper-anxiety, whenever he was faced with an interview. I encouraged Guy to think creatively. I asked him to imagine the part responsible for his fear as a symbol. Being a keen football supporter, Guy's was an appropriate symbol: a red card. I then asked him about what an empowering part would look like. His answer: a brilliant goal from a free kick.

In deep relaxation, Guy visualised the red card slowly floating out away from him and the goal floating in towards him. Guy followed this process each day for 14 days: inducing deep relaxation and imagining his positive symbol replacing his negative symbol.

What is really going on here is a clearance: out with the old and in with the new:

Internal dissociation with the negative
Internal association with the positive

Repetition of this process creates a ritual in training the unconscious to deal with perceived anxiety provoking situations in a positive way.

You are reconditioning yourself to have greater mental strength. Remember, it is your unconscious that controls what happens at the conscious level. What you feed into your mind is what your unconscious comes to understand as the real you and consequently this "new real you" is what manifests itself in your conscious mind and ultimately in your behaviour.

A couple of months later, Guy attained his first role with a leading law firm.

Perhaps you can think for yourself about an area of life where you really want to sell yourself but find it difficult. Maybe you want to feel more confident speaking up at meetings, or you want to propose some reorganisation ideas to your boss, ask the Bank Manager for financial help towards your new business venture – anything at all, as long as it is important for you. Recreate this situation in your mind and allow your feelings about it to come to the surface. Identify clearly any negative emotions that this process stirs up. Allow yourself to experience those emotions. Now associate this situation and these negative emotions with a symbol. The symbol you choose could be a colour, a shape, a feeling, a sound or an object. Once you are satisfied with your symbol, make a shift in your mind and try to imagine and feel what the positive and empowering emotions would be for this same situation. This may be more difficult to do, but much more pleasant, so persevere. Once you have clearly identified and allowed yourself to feel positively, again associate this with a symbol.

O.K. read the following steps and then have a go at internally dissociating the negative and associating the positive, using your symbols.

## Step 1
Induce a state of deep relaxation in the way you have been practising. Remember to take your time as your conscious mind is busy and needs to adjust gradually. Let yourself slowly melt from one state into another.

## Step 2
As you breathe out, visualise the symbol of unwanted behaviour and emotions to drift out of your mind, in front of you. Slowly, allow this symbol to change into the symbol of the empowering emotion. Maybe you visualise the negative symbol dissolving or exploding into tiny pieces, before the positive symbol appears. Maybe one symbol morphs into the other. It can happen any way you choose. This creative process will be personal to you.

## Step 3
Once the negative symbol has been exchanged for the positive symbol, as you breathe in, draw in the new symbol of the **empowering part** deep into your mind.

## Step 4
Repeat steps 2 – 3 six times. Remember to do this SLOWLY.

## Step 5
Awaken yourself from your deeply relaxed state in the normal way by counting up from 1 to 10. However before you begin counting up suggest to yourself that all parts of you will return to be fully awake apart from the part that you have dissociated. In addition you can tell yourself that you will wake up feeling refreshed, comfortable, and in control.

For this process to be effective, I recommend that you follow it daily for 14 days. Why 14 days you may ask. Well we need to give your mind quality time to make the changes needed. Remember the conscious mind deals with the logic but your unconscious mind, with which we are working, programs what takes place at the conscious level. You are working at a far deeper level and we want to ensure it has sufficient time to process the change.

On the next pages there are other creative techniques you can practise, which do not require such deep relaxation as the above. As a result, they aren't quite so powerful, but you may find them easier to execute and if rushed for time, they may fit into your busy day more easily. You could use them in tandem with the above if you wish.

## The Palm Technique.

Sit in a chair and relax. With this exercise there is no need to induce deep relaxation.

Look at the palms of your hands and think of a situation where you want to sell yourself, but where you are struggling to do so due to something that is a blockage within your mind.

In one palm (it doesn't matter which one) imagine a symbol of the part which is blocking you and focus on it. In the other palm, imagine a symbol of the empowering part, which will help you to sell you. If you find it difficult to see symbols try colours. Alternatively you may sense a feeling in the palms or even a sound. Go with whatever comes to you.

Close your eyes.

Now, bring your palms together with the empowering part on top of the blocking part and imagine the top symbol, feeling or sound diluting the bottom symbol, feeling or sound. Now bring your palms to your stomach and imagine the positive symbol flowing into you and filling your whole body.

Again, repeat this exercise daily for 14 days.

## Drifting Technique.

Sit in a chair and relax. With this exercise there is no need to induce deep relaxation.

Imagine your symbol for the negative part and see it or sense it drifting out of you and away from you into the distance. Remember once again this can be a symbol, feeling or a sound. See it travel right out to space until it disappears. Then, from the very same point where the negative part disappeared, see or feel your symbol for the good part coming towards you, until you absorb it and it becomes part of you.

Dissociation is one of crucial parts of the *You Selling You Programme*.

You need to have a clearance before you take in new stock. So, over the next 14 days practise daily one of the above techniques.

We can also borrow a technique that is often used to help those with phobias: **The Desensitisation Process**. This is a more advanced protocol to follow, however with practice it is quite possible to carry it out on your own.

Joseph Wolpe developed this model to help reduce negative psycho-physiological reactions to perceived and experienced difficult situations – otherwise known as phobic reactions to particular stimuli. In any particular situation, on a conscious level, we may be aware that we ought to be reacting in a particular way, but it may be the unconscious part of our mind (limbic) that contains memories and emotions along with automatic functions such as our heart rate and breathing patterns associated with the situation, that will govern the way we react. In other words, the unconscious program that has been built upon experience or imagination will control what happens at the here and now level.

Let's take an example of someone with a fear of speaking in public. They may be able to rationalise that there is nothing to be afraid of, that they are competent about the subject matter, that what they have to say is well researched and interesting, but even so they react in a negative way. They worry, they become anxious – sometimes to the point that this affects their competence or it may even lead them to avoidance of public speaking. This worry may have been caused by a bad experience in the past, or maybe just because they imagine something will go wrong.

In order to change the unhelpful conditioned response, the unconscious mind needs to be reprogrammed. Wolpe suggested systematic desensitisation: this involves a person imagining a number of conditioned responses to their "challenging situation" and merging them with relaxation and calming techniques. It is impossible to feel relaxed and anxious at the same time: what this process does is replace one feeling with the other: this is known as reciprocal inhibition. Blending relaxation with the anxiety-provoking situation will help reduce the anxiety associated with that situation. In addition, when experiencing deep relaxation, in the alpha brainwave state, the link between the "challenging situation" and the unhealthy response to it will be broken down.

If you choose to use this process, you need to be aware that you will experience the same anxieties as you imagine the situations as you experience in real life. So only attempt this technique if you are prepared for this. In addition, if you are dealing with severe anxiety, always talk to your G.P. first. Should you go ahead with this technique, it is important to remember to take your time.

## How to Desensitise:

Construct a scale known as a "Standards Units of Disturbance Scale" (SUDS). The SUDS scale is a continuum of 0 to 100.

e.g.
```
0    10   20   30   40   50   60   70   80   90   100
| ---- | ---- | ---- | ---- | ---- | ---- | ---- | ---- | ---- | ---- |
```

- sounds complex but in practise it's quite straight forward.

Now think of the specifics of a situation that triggers your unhelpful anxious reaction and plot them on your scale between zero (no anxiety or disturbance) to 100 (most disturbance) e.g. maybe you are anxious about making business presentations, your scale may look like this:

```
0     10    20    30    40    50    60    70    80    90   100
| ---- | ---- | ---- | ---- | ---- | ---- | ---- | ---- | ---- | ---- |
                    asked to           wake              car       about to
                    deliver a          up on           journey     present
                    presentation       day of        to presentation
                                     presentation
```

Now follow this process:

1. Drift into a state of calm and picture a tranquil scene.
2. Picture the **least** disturbing scene from your scale. In the example above it would be "being asked to deliver a presentation." At 40 this is the least disturbing.
3. As you **picture** this scene, notice the anxiety this triggers.
4. Now let your mind go blank.
5. Go back to your place of calm.
6. Now bring back to mind your anxiety-provoking situation – you will notice that the feelings of anxiety are beginning to drop.
7. Continue repeating the above process until you can think of your disturbing scene with comfort.

This may take time to take effect and you will have to repeat the exercise several times over days or even weeks. Eventually though, the situation that triggered anxiety will now be able to be approached in a more relaxed state.

Once you have conquered the least disturbing scene, move on to work on the next one up. What happens here is that your mind begins to associate the different events with a state of calm rather than the current unhealthy anxious state. For further details visit www.hypnobest.co.uk

**Check Your Progress:**

1. Remind yourself of the reason for starting with mind dissociation.

2. What situation will you use to practise mind dissociation – what symbols will you use?

3. Make a note of where and when you will practise mind dissociation this next fortnight.

4. How will you reward yourself for your disciplined approach?

## STEP 3: AFFIRMING YOU CAN

During this chapter you will learn how to combine the power of affirmation with visualisation. Having spent 14 days reprogramming your mind to dissociate any blockages, emotional restrictions and those parts of your makeup that are not working in your best interests and which you no longer require, it is now time to lodge, deep in your mind, a significant source of power. This will involve influencing the way you talk to yourself – your inner voice. This is because when you are making changes in your life, it's important to change your self-talk into that which will support you in what you want to achieve, rather than that which will trip you up along the way.

Research psychologists estimate that the human brain has 10 – 14 billion neuron cells and each can store thousands of bits of information. That's a lot of information, because our unconscious mind records and stores what we think of our experiences, what we say to ourselves about those experiences, what we imagine about ourselves in the experiences and also our emotional reactions to those experiences. You could imagine this part of your mind started as a blank disc on which every one of our experiences has been recorded. But the recordings aren't objective; the recordings aren't of bald, neutral facts: the recordings show our personal pictures and interpretations of those experiences. In this way, we have created our own reality, which we have continued to interpret as the truth.

Each recorded experience reinforces this reality, this truth and subsequently, the way we behave. The unconscious mind will not make a judgement call based on what will help you. Instead, your experiences lead to habits caused by repetition. It is the function of the unconscious mind to handle necessary automatic functions (heartbeat, breathing, etc) but it also handles learned automatic functions. These learned automatic functions begin at the conscious level and through repetition sink into and become embedded into the unconscious. Unfortunately, our learned automatic functions are not always helpful or appropriate to the way we are now.

What's the betting the majority of us have a disproportionate stash of negative self-talk packed away quite firmly in those neuron cells? What we want is to make sure that the bits of information we are storing from our inner talk are going to serve us in the way we want and that's where affirmations come in.

Affirmations are a way of working within the mind to change negative pictures to positive ones, to replicate empowering pictures of ourselves.

Affirmations are quite simply positive self-talk and affirmations linked with creative visualisation will support a number of things including your:

- professional achievements
- goals
- new habits
- interpersonal style
- relationships, e.g. with your clients and your boss
- confidence
- personal projection including body image and movement

The words we internally say to ourselves produce pictures, which in turn result in emotions and feelings, which in turn affect our actions and behaviour. Let me illustrate through this exercise:

Sit comfortably and close your eyes. For a few minutes repeat over and over the following words in your head, "I am relaxed and calm."

What were you seeing in your imagination as you did this? Maybe you could see yourself in a tranquil location or felt a sense of warmth. Or perhaps you could hear the sounds of calm. Whatever it was, record your experience in your diary.

Now, sit comfortably again, close your eyes and this time repeat the words: "I am confident," in your head for a few minutes. What did you see, feel or hear? Maybe you saw yourself standing tall, poised and exuding vibrancy. Maybe you felt a sense of energy coursing through your veins. Again, record your experience in your diary.

Now repeat the exercise once more but this time put the two thoughts together by saying: "I am calm and confident." Once more record the experience, the sensation of how you felt or what you imagined in your diary.

What happens during this exercise is that, as you repeat the words in your mind, pictures come to mind, and with them the accompanying relevant emotions. Don't worry however if you had no pictures in your head: you may simply have experienced a sensation or a feeling.

Look again at the exercise you have just undertaken. You may have noticed that the language you used: "calm" "confident" were to do with how you felt. This is significant as what you are doing is grooming and strengthening your inner self and to do this requires us to access our feelings and emotions. Remember the analogy of the Iceberg in Chapter 1: if we are to change our outer behaviour, we need to affect our inner self. This is a crucial part of the strategy in developing your ability to sell you.

Let's now take a closer look at affirmations and what they are.

Affirmations are:
- statements about you
- expressed in the present tense
- always positive

Why you may ask? Well, the mind cannot process negative language in a way which can benefit you. For example, let's say you want to give up smoking. It may seem natural to tell yourself, "I will not think of smoking or cigarettes." But as you say this or think it, what comes to mind? By using these words you bring the image of smoking into your mind so in fact you are constantly thinking about the very thing you want to quit. Maybe you're eating too many processed foods or sugary snacks. You know they're not good for you and you decide to do something about this. You may say, "I will not eat biscuits." As your mind processes the statement it creates a picture of biscuits or maybe a sensation of their taste and before long you're reaching for the chocolate hobnobs. The point here is, for the mind <u>not</u> to think of something, it has to think of the something first, and then <u>not</u> think of it.

In addition, affirmations should be short and realistic e.g. it isn't realistic to affirm that you are **always** confident, better to affirm that you are confident in most things that you do. Affirmations should also speak to your emotions i.e. your chosen words need to provoke your feelings or emotions in order to help groom your inner self.

## **How to install affirmations.**

First you need to state what affirmations you want for you.

To do this think about what you really want to feel about yourself in a particular situation and identify in your mind how that will have an effect on you selling you, e.g. you may decide to affirm "I am calm and at ease" and you may wish to feel this way when you are dealing with customers or when you are selling yourself at a job interview.

Alternatively you may want to display a greater amount of enthusiasm when selling yourself during a presentation. The natural affirmation to install in this case is "I am passionate and confident" or "I am excited and enthused". By doing this you are charging up your inner state so that you perform well.

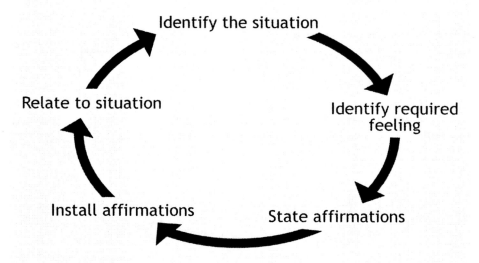

## INSTALLATION

1. In your diary, write down 3 affirmations NOW and identify the specific situation that these will support.

   e.g.

   | AFFIRMATIONS | | SITUATION |
   |---|---|---|
   | I am calm | ) | |
   | I am confident | ) | to support me at job |
   | I am at ease | ) | interviews |

2. Induce deep relaxation as you have previously practised.

3. Install your 3 affirmations – say these over and over in your mind, but not in a rushed or mechanical way. Do this 10 times (i.e. each of your 3 affirmations "I am calm; I am confident; I am at ease." 10 times).

4. Let your mind wander and see yourself in the situation you want to affect. Be aware of the sounds, smells, colours and feelings. For example you are walking into the interview room with a confident posture and a smile on your face. The room is light and airy. You reach out your hand and firmly shake the hand of the interviewer; you smile at and acknowledge the rest of the panel etc – but only you can really know the details as it's your situation no one else's. Enjoy this step, as here you are being who you want to be.

   Remember that when imagining try to do so actively rather than passively. In other words be in it. Feel, hear and see what is happening as part of you.

5. Awaken yourself from deep relaxation by counting up from 1 – 10 in the usual way.

Don't try to take on too much. Only work on one situation at a time: it allows you to focus and concentrate your attentions. However, you will find that just working on one area will have a knock on effect to other areas of your life and experience. In addition your emotional infrastructure will become more solid.

Let's take another example: a sales professional who wants to feel comfortable with her clients in order to create the right sort of rapport for successful sales.

Maybe her 3 affirmations could be from the following list:
I am confident
I am driven
I am passionate
I am at ease
I am focused

She follows the steps as illustrated above to install her affirmations. As she lets her mind go into the situation she notices her own posture, how she establishes excellent rapport. She sees her client taking an interest in her. The client looks and sounds impressed with what she has to say. She notices the desire she creates in her client for her product or service. She feels comfortable as she observes the natural dialogue between herself and her client.

I recommend you do the installation of affirmations for 21 days both morning and evening. You may ask why so long? Well, it is believed that it takes 21 days to establish a new neurological pathway i.e. to create a new habit. What this means in practical terms is that it takes around 21 days to transfer information from the short term memory into the long term memory.

Each time you affirm it is like watering the flowers of your mind or smoothing out those speed bumps. You are adding to the positive reprogramming of your unconscious mind. You can now relate psychology to neurology.

## How does the use of Affirmations relate to neuro-science?

Whilst there may be some disagreements between neuro-physiologists about how the different parts of the brain are related to different functions, one of the leading authorities on the brain and its functions, Paul MacLean, in his triune model, identifies the "middle brain" limbic system as the part of the brain believed to incorporate amongst other things: emotions, memory storage, habits and retrieval. The limbic system is also responsible for your autonomic functions such as breathing and heartbeat.

Drifting into relaxation, to rest the conscious part of the mind, enables you to bed down your affirmations. Replication enables the transfer of them to long term memory – that is, within your limbic system. I see the limbic system as your unconscious mind.

## Sceptical?

You may not be convinced about the power and place of affirmations and you're not alone. Over the years, some of my clients have been sceptical about whether positive self-talk can work. But believe me, my successful clients have been those who have embraced the use of affirmations. Your attitude towards them will play a part in determining what you can achieve.

Attitude in general will play a big part in moving you towards achieving your goals. With a positive attitude you will find you become more innovative, creative, and more fulfilled. The results in your life will be reflected in your own attitude. And remember attitude is a choice.

I can personally vouch for this. When my goal was to establish a successful business, my positive attitude towards this coupled with the use of affirming success led to a natural increase in my creativity and business achievements.

Conversely, a negative attitude automatically steers us away from our goals. So many times we prevent ourselves from doing what we want to do through the wrong attitude, so a change of approach may be crucial for us to develop and achieve our potential. Have you ever seen someone else's success and caught yourself saying, "I thought of doing that," or "I could have done that." So why didn't you? Could it have had something to do with your attitude, with your self-belief?

Take time to read the following quote on attitude. Notice how Charles Swindoll emphasises the point that what comes your way is often how you react to it.

## ATTITUDE

*'The longer I live, the more I realise the impact of attitude on life. Attitude, to me, is more important than facts. It is more important than the past, than education, than money, than circumstances, than failures, than successes, than what other people think or say or do. It is more important than appearance, giftedness or skill. It will make or break a company...a church...a home. The remarkable thing is we have a choice every day regarding the attitude we will embrace for that day. We cannot change our past...we cannot change the fact that people will act in a certain way. We cannot change the inevitable. The only thing we can do is play on the one string we have, and that is OUR attitude. I am convinced that life is 10 per cent what happens to me and 90 per cent how I react to it.'*
Charles Swindoll

## Check Your Progress:

1. Clarify in your mind what "affirmations" mean to you.


2. Why is it important to construct an affirmation in an emotional format?


3. Review your 3 affirmations and your situation. Are they right for you at this moment? Can you use these to practise installation with? If you wish change them, write your new ones in your diary.


4. Note when and where you will practise installing your affirmations


5. How will you reward yourself for your disciplined approach to installing affirmations?

## STEP 4: INSTALLING BELIEF IN YOUR BRILLIANCE OR "PUTTING YOUR WINNING STAKE TOGETHER"

Let's reflect on what you've done so far: –

- you've learned how to induce relaxation by engaging the alpha brain wave state
- you've begun to dissociate emotional blockages that have in the past hindered your progress
- you've installed affirmations that will help you to succeed

Each of these has focused on your Internal State. You have been nurturing and grooming your inner self.

The next step in the *You Selling You Programme* is to put all of this together and place the story of your success deep into the unconscious part of your mind, in other words, firmly establish the programme that will help you execute excellence in terms of your verbal and non-verbal communication which will lead in turn to helping you execute specific skills more effectively.

By carrying out the protocol that follows you are setting a specific goal and focusing on a result as though it is reality right now. When you set a goal a part of the brain known as the Reticular Activating System within the brain stem heightens your awareness to new information which helps you achieve your goal. In addition when you set goals that produce feelings of happiness your unconscious mind triggers creativity and focus to achieve the goal. The protocol that follows will encourage you to see the end result and have a vision of the goal as already in existence. This will also be planted in your unconscious mind so that your *creative unconscious* can automatically support you and take you to the goal.

Of course with any goal it is important to carry out the necessary practical tasks required. In other words there will be a partnership between your unconscious mind and your conscious actions.

---

Take Michelle, a HR professional in her early 30s. Although she had excellent professional knowledge and was extremely well qualified technically, she found it difficult to make the most of her skills for the benefit of her organisation. Something was preventing her from utilising her expertise. Michelle identified her goal. When she began to adopt the DIP protocol from the *You Selling You Programme*, within a few months she found herself behaving in a way that ensured positive impact.

---

Now, are you ready to **DIP**?

The process of putting your winning state together has 3 distinct sub sections.

1. **Define** with clarity a specific *You Selling You* vision of yourself.
2. **Identify** particular actions that contribute to this *You Selling You* vision of yourself: breathe life into your vision.
3. **Play** the movie of your success.

Let's look at each of these in detail.

## 1. Define The Vision.

Begin to create your *You Selling You* vision.

For a moment close your eyes and see a film of yourself being successful in a way you would like to be in a specific situation relevant to you. Imagine yourself clearly, creating a vivid visual image, but also add sounds, your feelings and even sense the tastes and smells if appropriate. Play this film and then freeze frame this still image, in your mind. Within your mind, see this as a success reality NOW. This enables your mind to conceive the success as already in existence. Remember the mind does not know what is real and what is not. Make it realistic. As you see, hear and feel your frame ask yourself is this exciting me? If the answer is yes stick with it. If it is no then recreate it. Remember to take personal responsibility for doing this. No-one can do it for you.

When working with sports people, I get them to define their vision. A footballer may see clearly his powerful strike, notice his accuracy and hear the roar of the crowd as he drives the ball forward towards the net. He sees, hears and feels the success. He sees himself walking off the pitch oozing success. I would then ask him at this stage to freeze frame this moment. Embedded into his mind is a freeze frame of success as a here and now reality. Therefore his vision is defined as a clear winner!

Or a tennis player may define a positive vision of herself as a superb accurate server. She may hear the smash of the racket on the ball and sense a feeling of triumph as she hears the roar of the crowd, as she serves the ace, and takes one step closer to game, set and match. This is the moment I would ask her to freeze frame. Why? Again because it is important the mind programmes itself for the end result. Once the mind is programmed for the end result it will creatively help you to automatically achieve it.

Practice over several days for around 15 minutes at a time drifting into a relaxed state and visualise your freeze frame. Also notice the feelings and sounds associated with the freeze frame. See the success as a reality NOW. This is your very own *You Selling You* defined vision for a particular goal.

## 2. Identify.

Identifying particular actions that contribute to the success of your *You Selling You* vision is essential.

Your still picture is not going to remain this way, as just a projected frame. You are now required to bring your vision of success to life again and begin to make it your reality. You need to pinpoint the specific actions that have helped you achieve this result.

Let's take an example of another sports person - a sprinter. Her freeze frame may show her standing on the winners' podium with a gold medal around her neck. She feels great, on top of the world. Maybe she hears the crowd cheer or her country's national anthem? Now she must begin to bring life to this vision. She starts to identify actions that have helped lead to this success. Her specific actions may be seeing her starting block technique, feeling the rhythm of her arm and leg movements during the race, her breathing technique.

Or what about the sales executive that needs to make a presentation on a new product to a group of clients. His freeze frame may show him standing confidently having closed the deal. He is smiling, so are they. He has heard positive responses to his presentation. He feels good. So what specific actions must he take that will ensure this scenario? He now starts to bring his vision to life. He imagines all the activities that contributed to his vision. This may include carefully planning his presentation, dressing in a way that will attract respect, noticing his confident body movement in detail. He may also notice the expressiveness of his voice and how this changes word to word or sentence to sentence. As he identifies the actions, his vision starts to have life. It starts to take on a dimension of reality. In other words he saw his successful outcome and then in his mind bought in the activities that made it a success.

Now bring back to mind your own freeze frame and start to bring the possibility to life. Remember, this is a snap shot of you in a particular situation, enjoying success right now!

Once you have defined your vision make notes in your diary of specific actions that can contribute to this particular vision of success. Look at the micro-contributions: what gesticulations you need to make, the melody of your voice, the intonation and inflections on words etc. Look at your body posture, its shape, clothes you wear, the facial expressions.

Now, take time to reflect on the specific actions you are taking that will make the *You Selling You* vision of yourself become a reality.

For 7 days drift into a relaxed state and allow your mind to focus on a different action you need to sell you. I recommend that you take up to a maximum of 3 actions a day in deep relaxation and allow the images you conjure to sink deep into your mind. For example, you may imagine your confident body movement, expressiveness and steadiness of your voice. These actions must be repeated in the mind so that in effect they become a conditioned reflex.

Of course it is essential that any actions placed in the mind are also carried out in reality. *You Selling You* is about both installing the success in your mind and also carrying out practical activities. For example a Business Development Executive who defines his success vision and identifies his actions would install these into his mind. However he will also need to make the conscious effort to cold call potential customers, and then put himself in front of the customer to attain the business. So relying on the mind alone will not work. It is a partnership of the unconscious programs you develop in your mind plus the practical logical actions you take that will produce the results. Practical actions are crucial, and the hunger to carry them out is equally important. As Henry Ford once said -"The harder I work, the luckier I become".

Working on your installation of these actions in your mind will automatically support your success when you put yourself in the real situation. With your mind not knowing what is real and what is not the good news is that when faced with the real event your mind will already know it can deal with it.

## 3. Play the movie.

Making it real is the next step. Having identified the vision of your success as a freeze frame of a possible reality and then the specific actions that are linked directly to that freeze frame, you are now in a position to see and experience your success as a full movie of reality.

Close your eyes and let your mind relax. Begin to play the full movie. Notice yourself successful. Pay attention to the environment, how you exude an image of success. Be aware of others responses, their encouragement, their respect. Avoid just seeing the freeze frame, nor is there a need to focus on each action – the work you have previously done when identifying actions should ensure that they are now integrated fully into your unconscious mind.

So reap the rewards and watch your freeze frame turn into a movie. All of the actions are now fused into the end result which is the freeze frame. See yourself achieving your success in this movie; enjoy the free flow of information between you and others, e.g. if you are imagining yourself on a date, see how comfortable you are, feel this, see your date responding positively to you. Or if your vision was to sell yourself in a business situation notice the way in which all the actions are naturally free flowing and how you comfortably achieve your desired result. In other words you are playing the actions that contribute to your ultimate vision as a movie of success. In your mind you play these actions up to the final freeze frame such as the athlete whose ultimate vision is the gold medal around her neck.

There is no limit to the situations where you can use the DIP formula. Maybe you are ready for a career move or perhaps you are managing a team wanting to inspire and engage commitment from your employees. Alternatively you may use the formula to inspire your business clients or even teach better in the classroom. But the programme isn't yet complete. You have begun to work on the internal elements of your make up, those which lie beneath the iceberg to support you selling you; now it's time to work with the external elements.

**Check Your Progress:**
1. Describe your freeze frame vision.



2. List the actions that will help you bring the vision to life.



3. Which 3 actions will you be installing into your mind first?



4. When will you begin?



5. How will you reward yourself for your disciplined approach?

# PART 2

# OUTER
# WORK

## Step 5
## Communication Excellence

## Step 6
## Lifting Your Personal Profile
## and Inspiring Others

## STEP 5: COMMUNICATION EXCELLENCE

Communication excellence is aligned closely to what Daniel Goleman refers to as Emotional Intelligence (EI).

In my view, EI is about developing two distinct components:

1. **Intra-personal Intelligence -** which involves your ability to be self aware noticing what is going on inside you, paying attention to those feelings and then acting on them appropriately.

   For example when engaged in a situation selling yourself you may notice you become tense. As an emotionally intelligent individual you recognise those feelings, pay attention to them, and act upon them. You may decide to take a few deep breaths to calm down to ensure you maintain your professional focus. In this particular situation you may also decide to deliberately slow down your pace because you are well aware that tension often leads you speak too quickly.

   Intra-personal intelligence is also to consistently build and monitor self esteem and confidence. Individuals with high EI will recognise times when their esteem level is low and take action to rebuild it using a range of techniques including those described in this book. In addition individuals with high intra-personal intelligence use their intuition. They take note and observe what is happening around them before triggering their external communication. In other words they use the green cross code, stop, look, and listen so that their communication is appropriate to the situation.

2. **Inter-personal Intelligence -** which is about how we communicate directly with other people. Your Inter-personal intelligence is determined by your

ability to adjust your communication style to create rapport, handle inter-personal difficulties, and develop and maintain people connectedness. This will be determined by how well you *naturally* listen and demonstrate empathy with people, communicate with the appropriate melody of your voice and at the same time ensure your body language is congruent with the words.

In measuring your emotional intelligence consider the following key capabilities of an emotionally intelligent individual:-

## Accurate Self Awareness.

This is your ability to pay particular attention to what is going on within yourself and with others when communicating. For example how well do you:-

- look at yourself in a critical light so that you can modify patterns of behaviour
- ask and listen to feedback from other people such as friends and colleagues and then act upon it
- listen to what your body is telling you and use this information when communicating with other people
- use appropriate non verbal communication signals to ignite the desired emotion on other people
- use your intuition to help you make decisions when communicating with a range of different people

## Regard For YOU.

This is your ability to accept yourself and value your true worth. When you do this you will find that you are much less critical of others and are more likely to behave in an assertive manner. This also applies to receiving feedback. If you have regard for yourself you will welcome feedback rather than becoming defensive. Ask yourself:-

- how well do I have positive inner self talk? If rare then work again on the exercises described in the first part of this book
- do I recognise that I have something to offer? Only drama queens will claim they have nothing to offer the world so take a moment to think about what you offer

## **Structured Goals.**

Making life interesting, stretching and fulfilling requires you to set goals that are realistic and specific. Not only this, but you should have timescales attached to them. Think about goals like this:-

- be clear about the goal in terms of what it looks, sounds, feels and even tastes like!
- be consistent in your efforts and actions to achieve them. This is aligned to the *You Selling You* DIP formula. Be consistent in your behaviours towards your goals and programme in your mind as if you have already attained the goal.
- when you set your goals make sure you take an immediate step to achieve them. Goals written and then put to the side will not bring you success.

## **People Connections.**

Your ability to build and maintain great relationships with people is crucial if you are to sell yourself. Consider asking:-

- how open am I with people so that I can build trusting relationships. Being open is the best way to create a bond with people. Of course you will have your boundaries but think how well you discuss and open up with people.
- do I show that I am genuinely interested in other people?

- could I go out of my way to support others a little more?

## Healthy Optimism.

This is your ability to have a bank of healthy optimism so that when the going gets tough you can reframe the negative and move forward. Healthy optimism however also means to control optimism. There are occasions when being overly optimistic is not appropriate. Ask yourself:-

- do I positively reframe the negative? If not then start!
- do I catastrophise situations? Again being a drama queen will not move you forward.
- am I monitoring my language so that I avoid saying things such as "that would never work" or "I could never do that."

## Handling Inter-personal Conflicts.

Your ability to manage conflict with other people will mean you can handle difference of opinion more effectively. Your state of mind to do this is massively strengthened by the exercises you carried out in the first part of the book. Handling inter-personal conflict will be achieved by people who:-
- have self worth so that they respect both themselves and others
- listen and empathise with others
- are assertive rather than aggressive or submissive

I recall reading in a management journal that EI is now more important to organizational and business success than IQ by 4:1. Clearly the same importance can be attached to EI in the process of *You Selling You*.

Just consider two individuals: one has a high IQ, but a low EI and consequently, poor social skills; the other has a reasonable IQ, but a high EI with well formed social skills.

92

Despite the high IQ of the first candidate, it is likely that the second is far more successful in many areas of their life.

When your Internal State is groomed and in good shape, your outer signs of communication will automatically become more powerful and the quality of your external communication will be better. This is good news. Think about it: it's impossible not to communicate to others - even when you're stood stock still and completely silent.

Consider a couple that have just had an argument and are not speaking to each other. Imagine them in their living room– seated as far away from each other as they can get. She pretends not to see him, as if he isn't there, but it would be clear to anyone observing that she does this in a way that will attract his attention. He, for his part, sits totally still, watching her with a pleading expression on his face; he tries to catch her eye so he will be able to see what she is thinking and feeling. Their communication is invisible: no word or gestures, but they are still clearly communicating.

What happens then? Do they make up? Practise using your imagination and finish the story yourself.

Even when we are not in such an intimate relationship with others, we are still communicating something to them: they are interpreting messages from us – we give out signals about our emotional state and we trigger an emotional response in others, even if it is one of complete indifference.

It is vital, therefore, that we are aware of what we are communicating to others, when it is important to us and how our communication is received.

**The way we communicate is the basis of the power of our influence.**

Why is this?

Well, what we communicate externally, not only creates perceptions of us in others, but also triggers emotions within the recipients of our communication. Over the last few years, after spending time training leaders to develop themselves from within, I have gone on to coach them on their external behaviour and to think about how they communicate and those who they will be communicating with. I have asked them to consider what thoughts and feelings they want to encourage in their staff, e.g. a leader may want to inspire and lead their team through change. Taking this example, he may need to think first of the emotions he wants to provoke and ignite in his staff, which will allow what he wants to achieve to happen successfully. He may want his staff to feel a sense of excitement about the change or to feel a sense of security. These emotions will make his staff more receptive to what he has to say; they are more likely to feel positively about the proposed changes and consequently their own behaviour will reflect this, being helpful and effective during the change process.

The feelings you decide to encourage in others should be ones that will help you to achieve the goals. They could be feelings of commitment, a sense of hunger to achieve results or even fear.

Hang on. Did I say "fear"? Well, yes. But let me explain. I am not advocating that, as a successful individual, you will want to or need to instil a feeling of fear in others. I am not condoning bullying. What I am pointing out, however, is that on some occasions "fear" may be an appropriate emotion for you to provoke.

e.g. imagine a leader who has a team in which there is a great deal of negativity, which is proving detrimental to business. Some staff within that team may need to realise that continuation of their negative behaviour may affect the business to such a degree that the business can't survive or thrive.

The "fear" which the leader may provoke is simply a result of staff becoming aware about the likely consequences of their continued actions.

Or perhaps take the customer who explains that they cannot afford an advertisement campaign to the sales consultant. It would be appropriate in this scenario to engage an emotion of fear initially by encouraging the customer to think of the consequences of not advertising. Perhaps the customer explains he cannot afford to advertise because business is very quiet. The sales consultant then asks questions such as "how much quieter do you think it may become?" or "do you consider your competitors will continue to take your customers?". By asking such questions will trigger a sense of fear and anxiety in the customer. Fear and anxiety often motivate human beings to act, hence the sales consultant will probably be able to move on to show his solution as a medicine to cure the fear!

Take the trouble to think carefully about the emotional response that will help you most to get what you want. Once you have identified the emotions you want to create in others and you're sure that they are appropriate to the situation then you go ahead and create them through External Communication Signs or Cues. In order to be effective and impress on others, these need to be:

Animated
Enthusiastic
and even Flamboyant

Because of the Inner work you have done, you will find you are becoming more comfortable and have greater versatility when executing personal behaviours that will trigger emotions in the recipients of your communication, which is conducive to achieving your desired result.

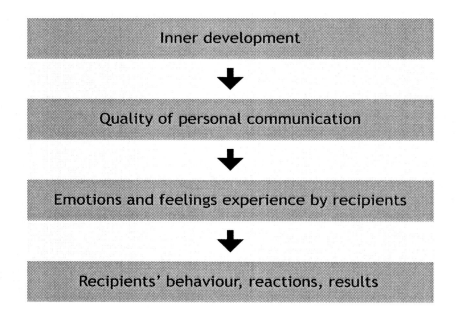

Thinking through the emotions and feelings you want to trigger in the recipient of your communication is vital. It is emotions that will determine the quality of your business results, the way others perceive you, your profile and ultimately the way forward.

This is especially true of sales and business development professionals. Referring back to how the brain is structured it is imperative that sales people trigger the limbic system and not just the cortex. Sales people hitting the cortex of the brain simply hit the logical thinking process of their customer. What they need to do is trigger the emotion of the customer. As you are aware, emotions are stored within the limbic part of the brain. This is why in sales training I stress the importance for sales and business development professionals to monitor their communication style and change it accordingly to trigger desired emotions. *It is the melody of communication that makes the real difference.*

Tony sold advertising and media solutions. He came to see me for one to one coaching to help him attain more business for his company and exceed his targets. First we explored what emotions he wanted his clients to feel so they would be influenced to buy not only the product, but also Tony himself. He explained he wanted them to feel confidence in him, to trust him and be inspired by him. As well as supporting Tony in developing his internal state, we decided that in order for him to be able to influence his customers in the way he had described, we needed to work on his external communication so that he could more easily provoke these emotions in others. This included him learning to display: an upright posture, a stronger and more expressive voice, and better eye contact to help draw his clients to buy him as well as the product. It meant him learning to move his body in ways that would be congruent with the words he used. Tony found this work led to him being able to use his skills to maximum effect.

After 6 weeks Tony contacted me to let me know he was one of the top sales professionals in his company and he was obtaining greater job satisfaction from what he did.

As you read, remember that the *You Selling You Programme* has two complementary aspects:

**Inner + Outer**

Work on both is necessary to ensure success. Work on your Inner self provides a strong foundation for and influences your External behaviour and your External behaviour reinforces and influences your Inner self.

**Inner + Outer = Outcome.**

We also need to pay attention now to the specific signs or cues of our External Communication. Whilst you may find that these begin to be more effective automatically as a result of the Inner work, conscious focus on our behaviour is a necessary next step in order to make the most of what we have and who we are.

**The specific areas we will address are:**

Posture, movement and gesture
Facial expression including eye contact
Voice, including diction, pace, inflexion
Style and Image

## Posture and movement.

"Stand up straight!"
"Sit up!"
"Don't slouch!"

Didn't your mother tell you these things?
Well, she wasn't wrong.

Our communications are reliant on the way we stand, sit and move. Through our bodies we illustrate externally to others our inner meanings and intentions and so it is important that we are aware of what our body is saying to others.

Maybe you should consider first how expressive your body is? Perhaps you've never thought about it, but you need to be aware that it will always be speaking volumes about you.

Take a moment and become aware of your posture now. If an observer looked at you, what would they be able to read from the way you sit, stand, lean, lie etc at this very moment? Would they say you are engrossed, relaxed, tired, worried, excited, cynical, bored, in pain, happy? It may be that as I asked you to become aware of your posture, you started to adjust it, becoming self-conscious of your body. The fact is, we don't usually pay much attention to this aspect of our behaviour– we adopt postures automatically, but I'm suggesting that to make the most of your communications, you need to pay attention, be aware of what your body is doing and consequently saying. Helpful posture and effective movement can be learned, absorbed and eventually become automatic to you.

Through learning to be calm, you have already gone some way to helping improve posture. Having a calm state of mind and a rested body, means that you can comfortably hold yourself with ease, allowing your body to move in a manner that oozes vibrancy and an aura of confidence and in a manner that is congruent with what you are trying to get across to others.

One fascinating way to develop your awareness of posture and movement is to observe others. Watch them stand, sit, walk etc. Ask yourself what response their behaviour stirs in you – not their words, their behaviour.
Consciously try out different postures:

- hunch your shoulders
- relax your shoulders
- walk around the room shuffling your feet, now change so that you feel you are gliding – maybe imagine you are walking down the red carpet into a Hollywood film premiere; now creep around the room; once again walk tall, stride out confidently
- try sitting in different ways – on the edge of your seat; with your legs crossed; with your legs stretched out; taking up as much space as you can; taking up as little space as you can

Just to show you how important relaxation is for movement and posture, try the following exercises: tense your shoulders and now walk around the room – you probably feel awkward and wooden. Now relax your shoulders, but tense the muscles in your buttocks and again walk around the room – if you can. Try the same exercise but tensing your feet. Of course in these exercises, we are exaggerating, but tension in our shoulders, lower back and sometimes our feet, is not uncommon and whilst our posture and movement will not be affected as much as in the exercises, they will be hindered by any unnecessary tightness in our muscles.

What is particularly fascinating is that, besides our inner state affecting our outer behaviour, our outer behaviour, in turn, can affect our whole psychology. Outer tension can inhibit our imaginations, our clarity of thought. As you carry out some of these exercises, try to be aware if your posture and movement affect your inner state. As you shuffle around do you feel differently to when you stride out and walk tall?

A great way to start feeling your body as fluent, fluid and expressive is to try the following exercise Stanislavski suggested to his actors. Imagine you have a drop of mercury on the tip of each of your index fingers. Gradually feel the "mercury" move throughout your whole body: feel the mercury run up and down each finger, then into your palms, up your arms to your elbows, then up to your shoulders and so on. You will find this helps to loosen the muscles so that your body movement becomes less rigid.

Let's see now whether we can take the above ideas about posture and movement and apply them to situations that are important to you. Imagine meeting a business client for the first time. See yourself with a positive, upright yet relaxed posture. What emotions do you want to trigger in your client? Perhaps it is confidence in you, trust and belief. You would like your client to think, "Yes I want to do business with that person." See yourself walking towards your client. What posture and movement will elicit the desired response?

Repeat the exercise, but imagine yourself as a client – see a potential business contact approach you. First see them with a sloppy, hunched posture, slightly tense and consider what this provokes in you. Now see them as upright and relaxed – their movements fluid and confident.

A colleague of mine told me of a car salesperson she had been impressed by. What had clinched the sale was not what features the car had, but the manner in which the salesperson had acted. He had appeared relaxed, but focused on his client. His posture was upright, welcoming and open. In fact he did little talking but his body oozed professionalism. My colleague explained she felt a high degree of confidence and trust in the man – and has since that first sale, returned for subsequent sales.

Posture, along with movement, can inspire professional trust. However, get it wrong - look like you lack confidence, show little interest, move in a way that is wooden - and you will easily lose out on opportunities and this will restrict your business relationships.

## Gestures.

When we communicate in writing, we sometimes choose to emphasise and stress words and phrases by underlining them, printing them in italics or bold font. In oral communication, gestures can help serve the same purpose; they can add colour and depth of meaning to what you have to say. Gestures can help you make your case more effectively, more persuasively, more sincerely.

Part of your work in *You Selling You*, is to ensure that your gestures are reinforcing your verbal messages and not working against them, e.g. if you shake your head whilst saying "Yes" or nod it as you say "No" what are you actually communicating?

Another important thing about gestures is that they should have a purpose and that they associate closely to the purpose and content of your verbal expression. Don't make gestures simply for the sake of making gestures: make them because they help you communicate what it is you intend to communicate.

Let me give you some examples of what I mean. Take for instance the sales professional selling advertising. Discussing what her company can do for her client she may say: *"our advertising solution will certainly help you drive your business growth <u>and lift revenue</u>."* On the words *"and lift revenue"* it could be a useful gesture for her to slightly raise her right or left arm, palm up. Her visual communication reinforces the content of her verbal message, thereby increasing its impact. This can be called **a double-bind communication.** Her body is therefore congruent with her verbal communication.

Now imagine a leader in business giving a motivational talk to his teams. His business has been enjoying year on year growth and as leader, he makes it his objective to ensure that this trend continues. He doesn't want his staff to begin to rest on their laurels. During his talk, he may say:
"...year on year on year, what we will do in moving forward, is to continue to accelerate commercial growth so we can all be proud ..."

Reinforcing, accompanying gestures could be on the words, *"year on year on year"* when his arm could scroll up on each *"year."* On, *"what we will do in moving forward"* his arm could point forward, then on, *"is to continue to accelerate"* his arm may move sideways. His arms could then move into his body as if he were embracing his team on, *"so we can all be proud."* Each of these gestures supports what he says verbally, they underscore his words.

Maybe a training consultant, at a meeting with her colleagues, wanting to emphasise the need to sell their service, says, *"what we really, really, need to ensure..."* where a reinforcing gesture could be used to emphasise the *"really, really"* – not only does her voice stress these words, but her gestures point them up further. She continues, *"...is that following a training course people walk out of our door feeling excited and confident that they can make a real difference."* At the end of this sentence, the speaker could point down, again reinforcing meaning.

This all may seem very mechanical, but inner preparation will often lead to automatic production of the appropriate gestures. This isn't guaranteed, however. Tensions, worry, habits, lack of clarity in our objectives can interfere with our natural behaviour and lead to lack of and/or inappropriate use of gestures, of which we are not usually aware. But we can help ourselves by becoming aware of our gestures. To sell yourself successfully, you need to know if your gestures are helping or hindering you.

By focusing on this aspect of your behaviour, you may become aware of fussy gestures, fuzzy or indistinct gestures, habitual gestures that don't help. Often these sorts of gesture e.g. fiddling with your lapel or a necklace, tugging at your earlobe, flapping your hands around aimlessly, are sometimes the result of tension and are nervous gestures. Clearly we don't want these.

Remember, that during a business transaction of any kind, our behaviour is more clearly spotlighted than when we are in casual conversation with friends, so any gestures will appear magnified and have greater impact.

What you need to ensure is that the impact that they make is a positive one; is one that helps you to achieve the result you want.

Remember also, that gestures are worth being aware of even when we're making calls on the telephone – yes others can't see us, but posture and gesture will influence the tone and quality of our voices.

So what are the gestures to avoid?

There are some gestures that will make it more difficult to sell yourself because the impact of them is far greater than the words you say to the other party. Typical non verbal gestures to avoid include crossing arms when engaged in conversation. Of course there are times when individuals do this appropriately such as when one is cold. However in conversation it is often unconsciously transmitted as a defence mechanism, i.e. a protective manoeuvre. One tip here is if the person with whom you are communicating with crosses their arms, mirror the gesture and then subtly begin opening your arms so that you lead the other person to a more comfortable position.

Other gestures to avoid include looking slouched for example when seated. Can you imagine the unfavourable impression you would give to the other person? The other person would notably feel uninspired and most probably dismissive of what you have to say. Also avoid gestures being too busy or when in a meeting such as a job interview gripping the chair as if ready for take off! Remember to sit comfortably back when seated. Sitting on the edge of the chair will make you create an impression of nervousness and a lack of confidence. Alternatively of course it could appear you don't want to be there so the other person begins to feel they are not valued and you are more interested in rushing off to do something different.

Finally I also remember attending a meeting with someone who throughout our discussion placed his hands behind his head. Not only can this make the other party feel uncomfortable it can be perceived as though the person doing this is wanting it to be made clear they have superiority. In you selling you avoid at all costs this type of gesture.

## **Facial Expressions Including Eye Contact.**

Similarly to the use of gestures, it is important that our facial expression supports our intention. e.g. consider what signals you are giving out if you smile when you give bad news or scowl when you congratulate someone on their success.

Practising relaxation will help you to express yourself more naturally through your face. If facial muscles are tense this will communicate itself to others and impede communication.

Imagine a sales person meeting a new client. They are feeling nervous and tense. This clearly will manifest itself in many ways, including, although maybe not obviously, facial expression. How can this sales person convey confidence and passion for their product/service? Not only that, taut facial muscles will impede animated expressions and also affect the quality of the voice. Tension in the face makes it more difficult to smile with both the face and eyes; something which can help put others at ease, inspire confidence and create rapport.

Eye contact and minute facial movements are crucial to communications. You've no doubt heard the expression that the eyes are the windows to the soul. It's true that the eyes communicate so much about you and that you can form a connection with another eye contact alone. To test out just how powerful this "invisible" communication is you may like to try out the following exercises, used by actors, but you will need a partner to do them with.

## 1. Mirrors:
Sit or stand facing your partner. Decide who is A and who is B. A begins to move – head, hands, feet etc – slowly and smoothly. B mirrors these movements. It is important that through the exercise A and B continue to look into each others' eyes; it is through the eyes that communication occurs, that the connection is made. As you continue with the exercise, it is possible that an outside observer will not be able to tell which of you is "leading" the movement. You will appear to be moving together as one.
Try again, swapping who leads the movement and who mirrors.

## 2. Echoes:
A similar exercise to the above is "Echoes". Again, with a partner, decide who is A and who is B. Sit facing each other and look into each others' eyes. A will then speak the

names of colours – red, blue, green, yellow, purple, brown, white – randomly, in any order, for as long as you want the exercise to last – 2-3 minutes is usually adequate. B echoes each colour spoken. Eventually A and B will appear to speak at the same time, as they will be so in tune. B can anticipate what A will say; there is "communion" between the two, with the main line of contact being through the eyes.

Eye contact is vital so try to smile with your eyes as this helps create rapport. How do you ensure you do this? Well try imagining that the conversation you are having is pleasurable. Smiling with the eyes can also suggest sincerity, inspire trust and induce a feeling of comfort in the other person. By looking at another person and really seeing them, you will help them to feel acknowledged. Not only that, our inner thoughts about that person will affect the impact of eye contact. Any negative thoughts will be transmitted through this "invisible" yet powerful connection, so try to think positively about the person with whom you are communicating – see them as a human being, and they will respond more positively to you and what you have to offer.

**Eye contact:**
- shows your interest
- helps you gauge their response to you
- shows you're listening
- shows you're confident
- helps build rapport and create intimacy

Conversely, avoiding eye contact communicates a lack of confidence in you, but worse perhaps can inspire a lack of confidence in others. You can also come across as insincere, untrustworthy and as if you are hiding something. If you find it difficult to look someone directly in the eye, you can cheat a bit and look at the bridge of their nose instead, as this still appears to the other person that you are giving them eye contact. Eventually, however, you should become more confident and eye contact should happen quite naturally.

**In your dealings with others become aware of your eye contact and its effects. Observe others' eye contact with you and how it affects you and your responses.**

## Voice.

Relaxation will play an important role in the quality of your voice production. If you are tense, your voice will suffer restrictions and you will not be able to make the most of this key player in your ability to communicate. Muscular tension restricts your chest muscles, your diaphragm and your facial muscles – these will all affect the sounds that come out of your mouth. In fact, tension in any part of your body can have a negative effect on your voice. You need to see your body as a musical instrument, say for example, like an acoustic guitar. The tone, volume and quality of sound produced by a guitar can be hindered if the body of the instrument is flawed in any way – same goes for yourself.

Everyone can have a great voice that is capable of expressiveness: a voice that can play a major part in affecting others. You need to ask yourself how good a voice have you got – how flexible, powerful, versatile is it?

Can you use your voice to produce a mood, a reaction, excite an emotion etc? Are you really making most of this asset?

To make the most of our vocal equipment, it pays to exercise it. The muscles we use to produce sounds are no different to any other muscles in the body. If we don't keep them in good condition, if we don't use them to their full extent, they become flabby, ineffectual and can't do the job they were designed for. Well, they still do a job of sorts – we can still speak and make ourselves understood, but we have no control over them, we find they will not respond in the ways we want when we need them to.

At times when we are relying on our voice to help sell us, say at an interview, a presentation or during a debate – we can find that we are let down. Our voice comes out thin, lacking power and conviction, maybe in a dull monotone. Work on your voice will help ensure that this happens less frequently. Try the following exercises, but first of all, relax, as this will help you get more out of the exercises.

1. Relax by tightening all of your muscles, holding them taut for 5 seconds and them releasing them; do this about 3 times, enjoying the waves of relaxation you feel. Take a few deep breaths, filling your lungs from the bottom up; try to avoid breathing shallowly with only the upper part of your lungs being used. You will know you are breathing with more of your lung capacity when you see your stomach rise before your chest does.

2. Now place your finger tips at the bottom of your ribcage and laugh and/or cough – although laughing is preferable. What you will feel is your diaphragm working, the muscle that is essential for breathing. It is this muscle that aches when you laugh yourself silly.

3. Now, as you breathe out, hum a mid range note. Where can you feel this note in your body? In your chest, throat, stomach? Repeat, but this time hum a high note and again feel where the note vibrates in your body – maybe you feel this note higher, possibly even your face or at the top of your head.

4. Repeat once again with a low note. Maybe you feel this note lower in your gut or maybe in your feet! Now imagine that your note is on an escalator, inside you. It starts high, on the top floor and moves down

through mid range to low until it is in the basement and then back up high to the top floor.

The following exercise is fun, but don't worry about looking daft. It will help show you that you have much more capacity in your voice than you may have believed. First of all say a few lines out loud, something simple, like a nursery rhyme. Now stand with your feet comfortably apart and flop over forwards from your waist, a bit like a rag doll. Now begin to swing your arms from side to side, like a monkey. On each down swing, breathe out audibly by saying, "Huh!" Get a good rhythm going. You needn't do this for long – try about 10 "Huhs." Now stand straight and repeat your nursery rhyme. Many people find that this simple exercise "frees" their voice and they acquire power and volume without strain or effort.

Sometimes our voices are less effective than they could be as we don't articulate our words clearly. Many of us slur our words, cut the ends of words and generally don't form our words well. To assist this aspect of speech, it helps to work the facial muscles. Here are some examples:

- mime chewing bubble gum and then blowing a huge bubble
- blow raspberries
- try to touch the tip of your nose and then your chin with your tongue – whether you do or not makes no odds
- smile as widely as you can, purse your lips, smile again etc
- try saying a tongue twister e.g. Red lorry, yellow lorry; Peter Piper picked a peck of pickled pepper; Sister Susie's sewing shirts for soldiers; She sells seashells on the seashore, or even, I'm not the pheasant plucker, I'm the pheasant plucker's mate, I'm only plucking pheasants, because the pheasant plucker's late

I'm sure you remember more from your childhood.

Let's consider some examples of how having well conditioned vocal equipment can help in *You Selling You*. Think of a Business Development Executive wanting to inspire confidence and create a desire in others for a particular product. The melody of his voice can help demonstrate his sense of conviction and belief in the product and for what the product can do for the client. The rhythm of his voice will contribute to the final outcome of whether he obtains his client's business or not. Once he can control his voice, and his voice is able to respond with ease, he can then find the appropriate melodies, and the appropriate rhythms that will communicate his intentions.

Remember a time when you gave a presentation. Was your voice clear, expressive, and articulate? Were the tone and pace of it varied? What was the volume like? It's no good if someone has to struggle to hear you and equally uncomfortable if someone has to listen to you shouting, or straining your voice. As you delivered your message, your ideas, were you able to trigger emotions in your listeners and were you able to retain their interest?

Similarly, in an interview situation, the quality of your voice and its rhythm can create interest in you and what you have to say; it can inspire confidence in you; it enables you to articulate your ideas and views fluently. Your voice will say a lot about who you are.

## Pauses.

Pauses are an important part of speech as they help break up what we have to say into manageable parts. Speech that rambles on without pauses can be hard for a listener to follow and can become meaningless. Some pauses, however, do more than simply organise the content of our speech and are more to do with the mood and effect you want to create. They can be used to draw people in to what you say, to grab their interest and keep it. They can create tension, excitement, provoke thought and can also help emphasise aspects of what you want to say. Never be afraid of silence – use it.

**Emphasis, pace and timing work together to create great effect.**

Let's look at the pause in action:

*e.g. **"What this will really, really ensure** (pause) **and this has worked for many of my clients** (pause) **is that -----"***

Here the pauses hook the listener.

You may have heard market traders attracting potential buyers to their stalls with their banter. Often what they say is amusing, but it isn't the words that grabs the attention of the public – it is the way they deliver their patter that does. Where they choose to pause, being a key technique.

It's the same when telling a joke. Poor delivery can kill it even though it might be the funniest gag in the world; yet effective delivery, with the right emphasis, pace, timing and judicial use of pauses can make us laugh at a mediocre joke, even one we've heard before. As Frank Carson used to say, "It's the **way** you tell 'em."

## Being an Assertive Communicator.

Everything we have covered so far about communicating will help you to be a more assertive and therefore a more effective communicator.

In the 1980s Assertiveness Training became the in-thing for professionals from all disciplines. It has continued to play a key role in personal development for those whose job involves working closely with others, and let's face it, that's nearly everyone. To achieve excellence in communication, it is necessary to be able to deal with a variety of situations assertively. An awareness of our own behaviour and genuine self confidence are important for our assertiveness. The *You Selling You Programme* so far has helped develop both of these aspects.

But what exactly do we mean by assertiveness and why, if it is the most effective way to communicate, don't we do it naturally?

In dealing with situations, we have a choice of approach:

Aggressive
Passive
Assertive

All too often we find ourselves behaving other than assertively. When we feel threatened by a situation – and that includes situations that make us feel nervous or those we lack confidence in, we tend to react quite naturally either aggressively or passively. These are situations that create a degree of stress and consequently trigger the flight/fight mechanism. When we feel anxious or threatened our body automatically reacts in such a way that we are prepared to either fight or run away from the perceived danger. Amongst other things, our heart beats faster, blood is pumped around our body faster and is diverted to those parts of the body that will help us to run or fight; we breathe more rapidly, adrenalin is released. This reaction happens if the danger is real e.g. an out of control car comes hurtling towards us or if the danger is only perceived e.g. we have to give a presentation to our staff.

Clearly in the first instance our life could be in danger and the flight/fight reaction may well save it. In the second instance though, the danger is less obvious – our life isn't in danger, but for some reason, we feel threatened and our body still triggers a similar, though maybe not as strong, reaction. In this case the flight/fight response isn't going to be very helpful: during the presentation we may well come across as aggressive (fight) or totally lacking in confidence and weak (flight). We may be so passive that we try to avoid the situation altogether.

## Learning to be Assertive is the Answer.

Being assertive isn't about getting your own way, as one client suggested to me. But it is about stating clearly and calmly what it is you want or would like to happen. Sometimes this may not be the result – you may still not end up with the situation as you'd ideally like it, but in the process of being assertive, you will feel good that you were able to stand up for your views, rights, opinions etc, without resorting to behaviour that tramples over others (or yourself) and the relationships you've built up. In many instances, being assertive will cement relationships, earn you respect and often produce a result that is conducive to all involved.

Just to clarify the differences between the three options of behaviour:

**Aggressive Behaviour** is that which we display when we want to get our own way. We think only of our own desires and needs and completely ignore those of the other party. Sometimes this behaviour works – short term. We may get what we want, but at what cost? Put yourself in the place of the recipient of this behaviour. If we feel bullied, badgered or coerced into buying something, agreeing to an idea etc we feel resentful, we lack respect for the person who has made us feel like this. We may not want to do business with them again or we may later sabotage their efforts. I remember when there was a plethora of sales people trying to convert energy users from British Gas to one of the new suppliers – one door-step salesperson came across in a very pushy manner; he almost suggested that because the new deal was so good I'd be stupid not to change supplier. I resented the implication, in fact I felt outraged that someone on my territory should speak to me like this. His aggressive ways simply triggered aggression in me and I told him where to get off – obviously I decided to remain with British Gas! Perhaps this salesperson was successful in some cases – he probably had targets to meet – maybe other potential customers were cowed by his manner and reacted passively, but not a good basis on which to start a business relationship. Ultimately I wonder how many of the customers he signed up he actually retained.

When we communicate aggressively it shows in our voice and body language. We don't necessarily have to be shouting and thumping the table with our fist. Aggression in the business world is much more subtle than that. It can manifest in eye contact that is held too long, pointing a finger, a sarcastic tone of voice – but most of all by not listening to others.

**Passive Behaviour** is what we show when we put others wishes and views before our own – in fact we completely ignore our own opinions and needs. We let others walk all over us and this not only makes us ineffective but it's down right unhealthy too. If this is the way we communicate regularly then we aren't going to be effective in business or in our personal lives. It is unlikely that we will progress up the career ladder - would we be able to sell ourselves to an interview panel? Would we put ourselves forward for promotion in the first place? We disrespect ourselves when we behave passively and this leads to low self-esteem and often a slow burning deep seated anger.

You may think that passive people are "nicer" than those who are aggressive, after all they let others have their own way, but they don't earn respect. Often, a passive person will suddenly become aggressive as a result of pent up disappointment and anger.

Passive behaviour may manifest itself in lack of eye contact, excessive apologising, closed/defensive body language, lack of fluency etc. and most of all they are often not listened to.

**Assertive Behaviour** is when we stand up for our own rights/needs, whilst acknowledging those of others. We listen and are listened to. Our body language and voice is helpful: we are at ease, comfortable, speak fluently, use eye contact and open gestures. Our voice – the volume and tone - match what it is we are saying. We show respect for others and are in turn respected. Assertive behaviour is made more attainable by the inner work you have already begun to undertake. Once our esteem is at a healthy level, respect for ourselves and others happens quite naturally. Consistent work on our internal state, will help lead to assertive communication.

In being assertive it is useful to follow 3 simple steps.

Firstly it is important that you actively listen to what is being said and show the person that you understand and appreciate their point of view. By doing this you are demonstrating an empathic response. This of course does not mean you necessarily agree with them but that you recognise their point of view. This step forces you to focus fully on the other person and not to become defensive.

Secondly you state what you think or feel. It is usually appropriate to start this off with an "I statement". This is your opportunity to state calmly and clearly your own point of view. For example the sales professional may explain "So what you're saying is you have a concern that our price is higher than our competitors." By doing this the sales person is reflecting back the concerns of the customer therefore demonstrating empathy. Following this the sales person will go on to explain his own point of view using the "I statement". This may be for example "however I believe that you will find that we offer a high quality product that provides value for money." In step two you are stating your thoughts and feelings without insistence or apology. When training people to become assertive I often recommend them to use the word HOWEVER as a linking word between step one and two. I am well aware that this may become a little mechanical so alternative link words may be used such as *nonetheless, alternatively, on the other hand, even so, etc.*

Thirdly you then conclude the conversation saying what you want to happen. This is essential so that you can explain clearly what you want to see happen without becoming hesitant or aggressive. However one must note that in life you will not always conclude with your favoured action. Often there is a need for negotiation and compromise.

So to summarise:

When we behave aggressively, we put our own needs, views etc first and totally disregard those of others. This behaviour will not sell you in a good light even though you may achieve short term gains.

When we are passive we put others' needs, views etc first and ignore our own. Again this is not a conducive behaviour for selling yourself. If you consider yourself to be a submissive individual then continue to work on the exercises described earlier in the book to boost your self esteem.

When we are assertive we are clearly aware of, and stand up for, our views and feelings etc but also acknowledge and respect those of others: we go for a win-win situation. This style of communication is far more likely to result in you being respected and help you gain personal credibility.

## Personal Image.
There are 3 areas we consider to do with personal image:

- the dress check
- the grooming check
- the body check

According to Lindsey Gibson, a leading stylist and image consultant, it is important to aim high in developing your personal image. In business she claims there is no such thing as to be too professional in one's appearance. Over the years she has worked with television personalities, news readers, company directors and even members of orchestras supporting them in developing a sharp professional image that promotes their ability to sell themselves whilst carrying out their professional duties.

Getting the basics right is crucial in promoting a great image and making the most of your budget and your shape is critical. I recall a time during a coaching session where it was important to discuss how to build a positive personal image. My client was unaware that whilst she had great abilities that her personal physical image let her down. She wore clothes and colours that in my view made her look dowdy and her hair was mangled with little care. Discussing issues around personal image is obviously a delicate issue so sensitivity needed to be taken. My client however welcomed the opportunity to identify actions of how she could fuel her personal image building. At our next session the following month she explained how she had employed the service of a personal stylist. This was evident in her new look. Not only did she look more polished and professional but she was naturally more confident within herself. What's more she then explained how she wanted to work on a weight control campaign. For the next few months she did just that and went on to become one of the most successful employees within her company.

Let's look at the three key areas of maximising your personal image, although you will find that they overlap in many ways and also relate back to some of the things we explored when discussing posture, movement and gesture.

## **Dress.**

Whether we like it or not, our clothing and style, including the colours we choose to wear create a perception in others about us. You may have heard others say, or said so yourself that, *"it shouldn't matter what people look like on the outside; it's what's inside that counts."* Unfortunately, noble though the sentiment is, when we first meet someone we judge them, as they do us, on appearance first. We see each other before we speak to each other – usually (although telephone, text and internet relationships allow us to discover what an individual is like before we can judge them from our visual impressions). There are always exceptions to the rules, but we are concerned in this book with helping you to sell you in the normal, everyday situations you find yourself in.

Our dress can often determine our professional credibility and is particularly important when you are selling yourself for the first time to an audience. My own view is that it takes about 12 more meetings with someone to change their initial perceptions of you – and if this wasn't favourable you may not get the chance to meet them twice anyway! Gibson explains that it is important to buy well fitting clothes and not ones that you are hoping to slim into. She recommends her clients buy good quality fabric to avoid creasing when sitting and to buy simple, plain, well cut garments especially when wanting to make a professional impression.

This all may sound basic, but the principles I outline are incredibly important on your first meeting with someone when that involves *You Selling You*. Your image and dress code will determine your "brand" – whether you are from the bargain basement or an exclusive, designer label. That's not saying you need to dress in designer labels, but you need to dress appropriately for your role, the situation and to impress.

Much of the advice I have to give regarding dress is pure common sense, but it's surprising how easy it is to overlook the obvious. Dress and style is also a personal choice, but there are some general rules that you may find helpful. Remember also that appropriate dress is only appropriate if it suits the occasion, the job, and the situation.

## Dress Check:-

- avoid creases – make sure clothes are ironed and neat. Linen is meant to be creased, and as a result is not always the best choice of fabric for a business situation
- wear suits that say you're a "professional"
- button up jackets correctly. When nervous and in a hurry, it's easy to button up out of sync – oh and that goes for remembering flies too!
- choose clothes for a good fit - not too loose or tight
- check with friends whether a colour suits you and the style does you justice
- choose a colour and style that fits the scenario in which you are selling you, e.g. unless you're going for a job as a lap dancer, don't dress even remotely like one
- navy blue – is a useful colour for the professional; taupe – suggests a softer professionalism
- dress in line with the emotions you want to trigger in your audience: clients, employees, senior staff, and interviewers
- make sure that shoes are polished and that their colour matches your outfit. Another thing about shoes and I'm really thinking of women's footwear here, is that heels, particularly very high ones, can affect posture in a detrimental way – remember the importance of posture in *You Selling You*. My advice would be to leave some shoes for partying.
- if your budget allows consider consulting a personal stylist. Details can be found at: www.yousellingyou.com
- for an interview, it may not be a good idea to wear something brand new – you don't know how comfortable you will feel
- if there is something in your wardrobe that you know suits you, looks good and makes you feel vibrant and triggers a positive state of mind wear it, if appropriate to the situation
- keep your wardrobe up to date

- have a clear out every now and again – get rid of anything that is faded and dated
- women don't need to dress like men to succeed

## **Grooming:**

Once you have your wardrobe sorted it is time to develop a personal grooming strategy. Let us take a look at what this means for you:-

- Consider your hair style – not everyone can handle their hair so take advice, often hair salons offer a free consultation. In addition maintaining the health of the hair is crucial. Can you imagine being in a situation where the dandruff has fallen on to your suit? Gibson always recommends to her clients that on a day where selling yourself is crucial that they book in with their stylist and let the stylist take off the pressure.
- Also I advise to control and consider facial hair – keep it trimmed and don't forget nasal hair. And control those long bushy eyebrows. A clip and pluck can often make the finishing touch.
- Hands and nails – keeping them clean, tidy, manicured and only the wedding ring. Remember when communicating with people your hands will be seen and there will be no contact apart from a possible handshake. Imagine attending a business meeting or a promotion interview with nails that look like you've been laying turf. Or maybe a sales person trying to sell his product with finger nails that looked like he'd just left a building site.
- Personal odour is another matter you must always be aware of. Remember that human bodies especially when under pressure perspire at a high rate so making sure you are well protected is crucial. Gibson explains that when working with television and film personalities this subject is an everyday challenge for them. She also explains that oral hygiene is equally as important although it is not advisable to chew

when in situations that require you to sell yourself. Keeping a spare breath freshener is always a good tip. Remember smelly breath speaks for itself and very loudly!

- Make-up can add value to personal grooming. But it is essential to avoid over use: keep it simple and natural. Consider taking advice from an expert.

## Body Check:-

Are you happy with you body image? Weight control is an area I've worked on with many of my clients over the years helping them achieve their ideal weight. It is always a good idea to seek a medical check up to find out your ideal weight range. It is then you can start to develop a weight control strategy.

One of the key objectives of millions of people is to lose weight, but I recommend you substitute the word lose for control.

Weight control means that you regulate the calorific intake to a healthy level. Fad diets tend not to work simply because they often do not show you how to maintain the weight loss.

Appropriate weight control is not just restricted to food. Your strategy must also include light exercise to burn off excess fat. Weight loss should also be gradual, with a recommendation for 1-2 lbs loss per week. Your strategy must also include a balance of foods to ensure you have a nutritional balance and make sure you also incorporate an increase in the amount of water you drink. One simple tip is to drink a glass of water prior to eating and sip water during the meal. Not only will this hydrate you but it will also satisfy the hunger.

In addition to the practical steps outlined above utilising visualisation and affirmations will always help you. See the body you want and place the image deep in your mind as described earlier. Be realistic for example regarding your height and bone structure. I have often asked my clients to sketch out on a piece of paper their ideal realistic body shape and to look at the sketch three times daily. This ritual becomes part of the affirmation process in itself.

In your relaxed state see your new "realistic" body shape. Imagine others making comment as to how good you look and at the same time notice how well you feel, how energetic you feel. Perhaps you see the admiring eyes upon you and the confidence you portray as you walk tall wearing the garments that make you look like a quality brand.

As you already know the unconscious mind will help support and re-programme your eating habits as well as supporting your personal motivation. Begin to see this as a lifestyle change rather than a diet.

## AND FINALLY Do you Smoke? Why You Should Stop Smoking NOW

Breaking the smoking habit can add wonders to your personal image. Not only will you reduce the risk of chronic bronchitis, heart disease, lung cancer, bladder cancer, emphysema, mouth and throat cancer and stroke but you will also contribute to improving your personal image in a number of ways.

By breaking the smoking habit you will lose the awful odour that accompanies a smoker, become fitter and healthier, and begin to notice an improvement in the texture of your skin as well as whiter teeth!

Your personal image requires action that ultimately makes you look professional, tidy, smart, and odour pleasant! Whilst it is all very well using the mouth freshener there is nothing more pleasing than to be in conversation with someone where there is no lingering tobacco smell, and to have fresh air floating between you so that there is no need to waft the arms around to move away the smoke. Most of all it also ensures that I can see you!

So how do you stop smoking? Well it may be useful to dissociate in your mind the part responsible for smoking using the protocol described in Step 2. Following this you may install positive affirmation that you are a successful non smoker or you are a confident non smoker. Because smoking is a conditioned reflex for many then the unconscious mind needs to reprogramme itself. Your conscious mind already knows that smoking is unhealthy and that you will have a better life if you were to stop. However that is conscious logic. It is the unconscious mind (limbic system) that needs to accept the suggestions that you are a non smoker. Clinical hypnosis is incredibly successful in treating the smoking habit in that it treats the triggers for the smoking itself. For example, often clients will explain that when they are drinking socially there is an habitual trigger to light up a cigarette, or maybe when faced with a traffic jam there is the need to open the packet and take a cigarette. If this is you and you want to stop smoking then you should consider clinical hypnosis to quit immediately. Further details can be found at www.hypnobest.co.uk

## STEP 6: LIFTING YOUR PERSONAL PROFILE AND INSPIRING OTHERS

Lifting your personal profile incorporates all of the pieces of the *You Selling You* jigsaw.

The first fundamental aspect of raising your profile is to understand how to influence those who you consider to be stakeholders in you achieving your goals.

### The Laws of Influence.

Over the years, I have read about and observed the application of the laws of influence. The laws which I consider to be essential in supporting individuals and helping them to achieve their goals, ambitions, targets and objectives include:

1. The Law of Reciprocity
2. The Law of Comparison
3. The Law of Consistency
4. The Law of Social Proof
5. The Law of Scarcity
6. The Law of Liking
7. The Law of Authority

Let's take a look at each of these laws in turn and see how they can be applied to help you raise your personal profile. You will, as you read notice the interrelation between all 7 laws.

### 1. The Law of Reciprocity.

When we are given something, we often feel obliged to give something back e.g. how often do we return a compliment with a compliment. The same feeling is evoked when for example we are treated to a champagne campaign, free gifts, a favour such as a word in someone's ear. Let me give you some examples of this:

When I was launching a business, one of my primary concerns was how to get a foot in the door of companies. I decided to enclose in the media pack I sent to large corporations a small bottle of champagne with the slogan "We're Fizzibly Different." Not only did this ensure that my marketing stood out from the multitude of others received, but the "gift" created a desire in the recipients to pay me back – at least with an appointment. This was all I needed; once I had passed the first hurdle of securing a face to face meeting with a company, I was half way there to creating more business. I had an opportunity to persuade, to influence and ultimately to sell the services of my company. It worked; from this one campaign I gained many contacts and an increase in new business.

A colleague of mine often organises conferences, which necessitate the use of coach hire. One company in particular is usually her first option, not because they are the cheapest provider, which they aren't. My colleague's reasons for preferring this company is partly because past experience has proved them efficient and reliable, but also because when she contacts them they have created a rapport with their client: they will ask about members of staff – they remember who they've dealt with before – their names, who's having a baby etc personal things like that. My colleague feels she is dealing with a company who are interested in her and her business and as a result she returns to their services time and time again. They offer a personal interest and she therefore feels obliged to stay with them; more than that – she has a desire to stay with them.

Another associate of mine, in conversation with one of their regular clients learned that the client was planning a holiday to Thailand. It just so happened that my associate had a good contact in the travel business and was able to point them in the direction of a good deal. It wasn't long after that the client was able to help my friend out in securing an interview with a company he had wanted to join for a long time. If you are willing to put yourself out a little and put in a good word for someone, then they are likely to do something for you in return – it makes them feel better; it creates balance: the Law of Reciprocity.

So go out of your way to do something for someone who you consider to be a stakeholder in your success, e.g. sending a card to or calling a client to help them or check their needs. I keep a little black book with details of client's birthdays, kids' names etc it helps me to remember when to send a card, or to ask how little Mary is etc.

Take another less subtle example: imagine you ask your boss for a promotion and he refuses; a month or two later you ask your boss to consider if you can go on a development course to support you in future promotion opportunities. It's likely that your boss will be amenable. You showed your boss respect by accepting his first decision and your request shows that you wish to act on it. By giving this respect, he owes you one and is likely to pay for you to attend the training course you've asked for. Or perhaps you go out of your way to help support a senior person. For example staying late to help complete a business project that has a tight deadline, or offering to help by taking some work home.

Of course be aware of over playing this rule. The last thing you want is to be known as a sheep or be seen as false. Use the rule tactfully but do make sure you use it.

## 2. The Law of Comparison.

Understanding how the law of comparison works can be extremely beneficial and can work in several ways.

This law is sometimes about comparing yourself to your competition. Large corporations do this all the time e.g. Tesco's do this as part of their wider marketing campaign: on their web site they invite you to compare their prices for certain items with the prices for the same items at other leading supermarkets. We often see claims and promises on the high street offering your money back if you can find items cheaper elsewhere.

On a personal level, say for example you are raising your profile for a possible promotion. Do your best to find out who else is being interviewed and when they are being interviewed in comparison to you e.g. say you discover that colleague Zandra is trying for the same position and you know that she hasn't much chance in succeeding – maybe she is too inexperienced. If you can influence the interview times, it may be useful to schedule your interview immediately after hers. Why? Because, in comparison to Zandra, your abilities and suitability will appear significantly greater.

The law of comparison also works in other ways. Imagine you are a sales professional selling media advertising. It would be wise to suggest to your client the most expensive advertisement option first. So you provide details and explain the benefits of one which is large, creative, and unique. Once you've shown that you can meet their main requirements, you then follow with information about cheaper add-ons such as a full colour option. The reason? Well, it's to do with your buyer's psychology. Let's suppose that the cost of the main advertisement was £2,500 and add-ons were an extra £250. If you had begun to sell the cheaper £250 add-ons and then progressed to selling the £2,500 main advert, the leap upwards in price difference is a bit of a shock and would more likely unnerve the client than had you started the other way round. Starting with the larger sum of £2,500 makes the cost of add-ons of £250 appear inexpensive in comparison. The comparison of prices creates a different effect on the buyer depending on which way round you present the comparison.

## 3. The Law of Consistency.

The law of consistency recognises that human beings like to keep their thoughts, beliefs and actions consistent with what they have previously done or decided. If you are employed in business development and sales, this law is of particular importance. In his book, *Influence: Science and Practice*, Robert Cialdini gives an example of toy manufacturers using this law. Prior to Christmas, he explains, toy manufacturers may use this law and advertise certain products: people expect to see ads for toys at that time of year. They may also plant PR stories about it being impossible to buy a certain product. They will then deliberately under supply shops to create demand (see Law 5 - The Law of Scarcity). At the same time of course, parents who have promised Ryan or Amy the toy, will be searching frantically to find one. Parents want to remain consistent to their promise, but of course the children are disappointed. Suddenly after Christmas these toys reappear on the shop shelves and continue to do a fantastic trade because this allows parents to keep the promises they made and be consistent.

Consistency is also applied when sales people apply the "Yes Set" series of questions. The "Yes Set" was developed by renowned hypnotist Milton Erickson.

This consists of someone asking a series of questions that provoke the answer, "Yes," thus putting the responder in a positive frame of mind. Let's look at an example when selling:

Imagine you are in a meeting with a client and you are trying to sell them advertising. They aren't particularly encouraging and say: "Business is slow at the moment and we're struggling; I'd find it difficult to spend money on advertising". So you need to convince them. By using a Yes-Set series of questions, you can condition your client to say "Yes." Maybe you reply:

"So what you're saying is that this is a difficult time for you to invest in advertising?"
"Yes."
"Because business is tough at the moment, I can appreciate that when you spend, every penny must count."

"Yes."

"So any money you were to put into marketing and advertising, we would need to be certain that there would be a probable return on your investment?"

"Yes."

"To meet that need, obviously we would need to ensure that your
product/service stood out in any campaign."

"Yes."

"I believe we could help you to achieve this and I imagine you'd be willing to consider our ideas?"

"Yes."

... and so on. What you have created here is a sort of ritual of saying "Yes." Clearly this is a hypothetical conversation and also you haven't yet sold anything. But you have given yourself a chance to do so when initially you were being turned down.

## 4. The Law of Social Proof.

If everyone else is doing it then we want a piece of the action. In raising your profile, especially if you are in the world of sales or business development, draw your client's attention to how their competitors are all using your product. Just think about certain fragrances, designer clothes or the latest personal gadgets that have been made desirable must haves after being promoted by high profile celebrities. In the early days of mobile phones I remember the desire that was created by people's need to have a piece of the latest trend. The social status was huge and to some degree still is with next generation phones being produced year after year.

How else can you use this law?

- think of the salient features of yourself. For example who have and who are you associated with? A friend of mine has no problem securing credit when she mentions a certain celebrity.

- Ensure you have on side influential stakeholders if you are going to an interview. Their approval and testimonial will go a long way to help your success. It goes a long way if someone respected has already said to the interview panel how marvellous you are.

Again be aware of over use of this law. It can make others see you as desperate and lacking in self belief.

## 5. The Law of Scarcity.

Have you ever been in a situation when you have wanted something but you know that its availability is limited - maybe you wanted a rarely available property in a desirable area, a limited edition car or even tickets for a concert. The scarcity of this product has led you to want it even more? Not only that, you are prepared to pay a higher price for it too.

The harder it is to acquire something, the more we appreciate its value.

*"The way to love anything, is to realise that it might be lost"*
*G.K. Chesterton*

How can you use this law?

First, if you want to impress your own clients and your product or service is in short supply – combine this with the law of social proof. Sales people can also use this law when they demonstrate to their client that they will pull out all the stops to help the customer get the product or service they really want. By doing this, the sales professional gains the emotional trust and commitment from their client.

In planning a career, identify specific qualifications that you recognise are in short supply by your organisation. Develop skills that decision makers are keen to acquire because they are in short supply. In one organisation I worked for, a promotion opportunity to first line management suddenly came available for a group of 8 employees. The senior manager wasted no time in encouraging one particular individual to apply for the post and indeed this employee gained the role. As is usual in these cases, there were some disgruntled members of staff who had not been successful, but I pointed out to them that what their rival had that they hadn't were skills that the employer was beginning to need due to new demands and a changing climate. Not only that, the successful candidate had foreseen this gap in the skill base and had actively taken steps to acquire those new desirable skills. She didn't gain her new post through one good interview, she had already signalled her desire for promotion through her actions and her suitability to fill the role. She had something that was in demand and scarce.

When I first started to build up my clinical hypnosis practice, working with clients on a one to one basis, I found that as I became busier and busier, it became common knowledge amongst my clients and potential clients that:

   a) I was good at what I did **and**
   b) I was successful

The fact that I was building up a waiting list helped. Because it became more difficult to get an appointment with me, then I must be popular, so consequently I must be good enough to wait for. The longer my waiting list, the more my time was in short supply, the more people wanted to use my services.

## 6. The Law of Intimacy.

Sounds interesting, but what is it? First of all, we tend to like people we are physically attracted to. You may say that's all very well but beauty is in the eye of the beholder – we are all attracted to different things. However, you can enhance your general attractiveness by simply following some of the advice on dress, grooming, body care and body language in the Communications section.

There is evidence to suggest that people who appear attractive to others, earn more, close deals with clients more easily, climb the corporate ladder faster and develop relationships more quickly. We also tend to like people who have something in common with us. Take your time to listen to those you want to sell yourself to. Making an assessment of what makes them tick, what their interests and values are can do much to help you judge how to deal with that person and make the connection of mutual interest. When selling yourself and creating an intimate relationship, take time to mirror the person with whom you are communicating. Perhaps mirror the style of dress common to an organisation when attending an interview or when meeting clients. We like people who remind us of ourselves, because this reaffirms our self-image.

In creating intimacy to influence others, we also like people who give us compliments, although be cautious of complimenting too often. Compliments are best when they sound sincere and natural, e.g. instead of saying: "I think you are very efficient," which sounds a bit stiff and formal, it would be better to say: "that's a good way of doing that – it definitely saves time – I'm going to try it." In addition people you are influencing want to feel comfortable. In training sales teams I have always developed them to present with an informal professional focus with a key objective of making their clients feel comfortable. Of course there are exceptions to the rule where the more formal approach is appropriate and you need to be able to switch your style accordingly.

Cooperation is something you should always strive for. Be aware when influencing others not to damage egos. I recall coaching a company negotiator. During our discussion he would reply to my suggestions "Yes I know that," "Yes, possibly," and statements prefixed with "Yes, but..." I asked him whether his style of responding to me was the same as his style when negotiating. He confirmed that it was. After learning to adopt a more cooperative style of communicating excluding the "yes buts" etc he began to achieve his ideal settlements with his clients much more readily.

We also prefer to like people who are positive. In lifting your profile, be very aware of you attitude. Take for example the senior manager aspiring to become a director. In a meeting with her to support her accelerated development there were times when she was openly negative about her organisation, its culture and direction. I pointed out that this would hold her back in aspiring to reach board level unless she reprogrammed her communication style. What she needed to understand was that people with a positive attitude are the ones we prefer to spend time with, work with, and work for. Ask yourself if you think her Chief Executive would promote her with a clearly negative attitude? So even though we may have knowledge, skills and abilities – they need supporting with a positive attitude.

## 7. The Law of Authority.

When we have personal authority, our ability to be perceived in a positive light and with respect, increases. I remember spending time visiting a relative in hospital and observing the communication – verbal and non-verbal – of other relatives when they spoke to different personnel. When Medical Consultants updated them on their relatives' progress, it was noticeable that they listened more carefully and accepted more readily what they were told, even if it was the same as what someone else, maybe nurses or auxillaries, had already told them. The appearance, the words used and the perceived status of a consultant influenced the visitors' behaviour. The Consultant was seen as an expert, so the belief was that they must have known what they were talking about. Sometimes people assume someone is an authority because of their age, gender, appearance or accent. Often people get it wrong and this can be irritating to those of us who are the authority. But rather than let this inhibit us, what we need to do is to impress on others that we are the expert. To do this, that is what we truly need to become. Look at the field you work in – research it, become aware of what's current, form an opinion and be at ease when discussing issues related to your field.

Your ability to influence and lift your profile will certainly increase if you are an authority on something that others want to know about. Can you develop an authority? Take time to reflect on this question and act upon it.

## **Making Connections with People.**

Often described as rapport, making people connections is to ensure that the other person can see, feel, and hear you giving them your undivided attention and making them feel special. Primarily this means you need to show that you **really** listen and take a genuine interest in the other person.

So what will it mean to gain connection with people so that you can sell yourself to them?

- firstly avoid the first impression often taken by many people that the other person is boring or dull. If you draw that conclusion then it is your task to find the interesting side! Remember that the thoughts you carry in your mind will be transmitted through your body language.

- always show an interest by using comfortable eye contact. Look interested as you look at the other person. And inside your mind tell yourself how much you really want to get to know this person. It is my belief that you will be subliminally communicating to the other person at the unconscious level making them feel special. Also ask questions that the other person will enjoy answering. Of course the expressiveness in your voice must also match the words so that the melody of your voice carries the message of – I am interested in you.

- matching and mirroring the other person will also help you gain connection. Matching means to subtly copy the body language, tonality, and words that the other person uses. When people match each other what they are unconsciously saying to themselves is we are alike, we have similar styles, values etc. Remember this is not manipulation, but indeed is a healthy way to gain rapport and people connections. Matching is often witnessed in life generally especially in laughter and yawning. Think back to the last time someone yawned and you replied explaining they were making you do the same. Mirroring the other person is slightly different to matching in that you would be, quite literally, a mirror image to the other person. For example as one person lifts their left hand you lift your right hand. Matching and mirroring can be applied in a number of scenarios such as the sales professional building a business relationship or the time you meet the perfect stranger and want to make sure that when the conversation has concluded you have definitely built a connection so you receive that phone call. Be cautious in overusing the matching and mirroring tool. I have witnessed too many times people practicing this technique to their detriment. Over and obvious use may mean the other person notices and suddenly yells, stop copying me!

## **Building your charisma.**

Having a personal presence is the key to building a charisma. You will have done a number of mind exercises already and these will certainly help you to develop a more charismatic presence. Why? Because having charisma is about having the right state of mind. Having empowering thoughts will lead to more positive feelings and you already know that this determines the quality of your external communication.

So how can you develop a charismatic presence?

1. Each day exercise your mind – Make sure that you do at least one of the exercises described in the first section of this book. The mind needs as much exercise as your body so practicing mind dissociation, affirmation, or the DIP technique will help ensure you are mentally fit.

2. Accept that you are fallible. Give yourself permission to accept that you are not going to be perfect and that is ok. Take the sales person making a prospect call. She considers she needs to know everything about their customers business, have an answer to every single question, able to overcome every objection and to close the sale within the first meeting. Imagine the emotional state of the sales person walking into the meeting. In all probability she will be anxious, ruffled and too quick in her communication style when talking to the decision maker. This style then leads to the meeting being uncomfortable, she forgets to listen and her decision maker feels he does not want to do business because the meeting was a disaster. If on the other hand the sales person arrived at the meeting recognising she knew enough but not everything and accepted she could answer many questions but if there was one she could not answer that was ok because she could find out, and then her performance would more likely be professional, calm, yet inspiring. Why? Because she allowed herself to be fallible.

3. Remember you are equal. I recall as a young person my first position in a telemarketing role. I performed very effectively and was always winning monthly incentives. One day the Managing Director of the business arrived to talk to the staff on the front line. Preparations were put into place to ensure the department sparkled on that day. The day she arrived I was asked to meet with her and provide an update on a number of projects. I was called into a meeting, offered a coffee and faced the Managing Director of the company who looked interested, smiled and said how much she was aware of my good

work. I suddenly became very nervous, and was desperate to make a good impression. It was as though I became a little boy looking at a mother figure. What I needed to do was relax and recognise that person as an equal human being and whilst I would of course respect the position and the person holding it I was also due respect and had something to offer. As you can imagine the meeting did not go as well as what I wanted. So remind and accept you are an equal. You are worthy of being listened to and have special strengths. Accept it!

4. Allow yourself to have a positive energy. This does not mean you need to be performing like a greyhound at the race course but providing passion about what you believe. Your passion may be for a professional purpose or to get more police on the beat in your local neighbourhood. Your passion for something may not always be met with the same enthusiasm but is more likely to be respected.

5. Earlier in this book I mentioned how your thoughts will be transmitted to other people at the subliminal level. As I write this book it was only yesterday I explained to a group of sales professionals that when they deliver a sales pitch to an audience to be aware of presenter paranoia. What often happens is that we can look at other people and conclude they are bored with us or not impressed. The best response in these circumstances is to transfer the thoughts in your mind you want the person or the audience to have. For example in your mind you may say "I provide you with enthusiasm" or "I provide you with intrigue". It is often useful to think in your mind what emotion you want the person or the audience to feel such as "I provide you with confidence" or "I provide you with excitement". You then begin to make the assumption this is what the person or the audience is thinking or feeling. This can be very powerful. Try it out.

## Networking.

It may seem unfair, but how often have you heard: "It's not what you know, but who you know." Who you know can be crucial to success, hence try to develop a network of helpful contacts. But what exactly is networking? It can be defined as the art of meeting people, building relationships with these people and gaining benefit from these relationships.

Networking is crucial if you are to influence those who have a stake in determining how you sell you. For example getting to know key players who can provide word of mouth recommendation of your product or service can really help lift your results.

I remember the time when I set up my first business. My priority was to attend business groups, have conversations with members and ensure I followed up calls having created an interest in my services.

If you are confident from within, you will be more able to create a positive impression and impress others. Networking will help open doors for you.

So how can you develop a strong network? Try the following guiding principles:

- Provide assistance to others
- Ask if you can help
- Take an interest in others' goals and aspirations
- Ask others for advice: arrange meetings with others - a little constructive cheekiness is allowed
- Ask others for further recommended contacts and when you talk to these parties mention who recommended them
- Carry business cards with you
- Be patient – results aren't always immediate, but that doesn't mean you are not making progress
- Be proactive and follow up opportunities

- Show you are interested in your contacts and that it isn't all about you

## **Modelling Excellence.**

Have you ever watched a young child mimic their parents? I used to often sit back and watch my niece copy her parents: she wanted to play at ironing clothes and hoovering the floor at the same time that these chores were being done for real. And when she was in the car she would copy the driver's actions. What she was doing was "modelling" behaviour.

Modelling is a process of observing how an individual does something and following the same patterns of behaviour yourself. Obviously for success, we need to model those who demonstrate excellence and achieve their goals.

It isn't simply a matter of mindlessly copying, modelling means you engage your thought processes too.

I was coached once by someone who I believe has the most outstanding talent for communicating, along with the air of a winner. I considered what it was about her that gave me this impression.

In our sessions I would observe her talent to articulate her ideas with precision, strength but also warmth. I focused on how she held herself – she seemed to glide through a room and carry an aura of confidence. I concentrated on this picture of her and how she executed her behaviour and it wasn't long before I found myself beginning to show these same positive behaviours.

During a difficult sales presentation, where I encountered a series of challenging questions, considering how my coach, Alice, would handle the situation affected my behaviour. I found myself speaking strongly, confidently and my body became more upright and animated – all this allowed me to reinforce my message. It was as if I had put on the "mantle of Alice." So how do you model excellence?

1. Identify someone who you consider demonstrates the required excellence.

2. Observe closely their behaviours. Listen to their voice – its expression, tone and even the words they use. Also be aware of their body language, their posture and facial expressions. You may notice how they carry themselves and how they engage in conversation to influence others.

3. Drift into a relaxed state. For about 5 minutes, imagine your model demonstrating effective behaviour – use all your senses to do this.

4. Allow your mind to go blank and then for a further 5 minutes, imagine yourself taking on the behaviours yourself. Try to be specific during this part of the process – notice yourself in detail. You may well find that simply doing this exercise makes you feel more confident and that your actual behaviour starts to change e.g. you have a more upright posture.

5. Repeat this process so that your mind begins to associate the behaviours of your model to that of your own. In other words your unconscious mind will programme itself so that when in situations requiring you to sell yourself well you will automatically take on the behaviours and actions of the model of excellence.

6. Having programmed this into your mind next time you are in a challenging situation, maybe an interview, a sales discussion, or a meeting with the boss think and picture in your mind how your model of excellence would behave. Automatically you will very soon begin to notice that you model his/her style which helps you get the result you want.

## CASE STUDY A

## DISSOCIATING OLD HABITS

When Liam, a 34 year old Business Consultant came to see me, his issue was one of limited self-belief. This tended to trigger anxieties within him, which in turn led to poor performance; it also affected his ability to inspire his clients to do business with him hence his professional results were poor.

He explained to me that reinforcing these feelings of inadequacy and feeding his sense of panic were increased by demands at work for him to improve his results.

He was living with a perceived threat: - that if he did not improve his performance quickly, then he would disappoint his managers and risk dismissal. He was caught in a vicious cycle; his anxiety prevented him from operating successfully and his poor results created a situation which simply made him even more worried.

After understanding his condition, I agreed a two stage process with him that put particular emphasis on:

1) dissociating the part(s) that were responsible at an unconscious level for Liam's poor performance
2) replacing these "blockages" with more empowering "parts." Something that would support Liam's ability to communicate with his clients in a more effective manner

In carrying out Stage 1) of dissociating blockages, Liam used the "Palm Technique" using the following protocol: as he focused on the palm containing the part to be dissociated, Liam said he "felt it – like a cold, heavy weight." As he went into the "Alpha" state, he was still aware of the heavy, cold weight in his palm. At this point, I explained to him that this part had served some purpose for him at an unconscious level. Liam then, using the power of his mind, communicated with this part/blockage. He negotiated with it –requested it to change or shrink. The process took about 5 minutes, after which, Liam felt the part from a heavy, cold weight turn into a warm, comfortable sensation. The part wasn't "light" i.e. it was still substantial, but not uncomfortably heavy. It felt solid and secure.

After this "negotiation" was completed, Liam brought his palms in towards his forehead and imagined the newly transformed part entering his body.

I met with Liam over the course of 3 weeks. At our next two sessions, as Liam entered the "Alpha" state, I assisted him in affirming his brilliance. I installed positive suggestions/affirmations into his mind at the unconscious level. I suggested he let his mind drift into the future so that he could feel, see and hear himself working with his clients and influencing them to do business with him.

A further 3 weeks after the sessions, I discussed the results with him. He said: "I just feel a surge of confidence, like I've never had before. It's amazing." He told me that he felt more self-assured when meeting with his own business clients; that his style of communicating was naturally more exuberant. Importantly, his ability to drive business contracts to a successful conclusion and increase revenue for his employer and himself had improved. Now Liam was in a different kind of cycle: the one of success building confidence to create more success.

He was no longer being held back by that cold, heavy DEAD WEIGHT.

## CASE STUDY B

## AFFIRMING YOU CAN

Tom, a 26 year old Advertising Sales Executive, was a good performer; in fact many people would be happy to achieve the level of his results and ask for no more. Tom, however, realised that he needed to carry on growing and improving – he needed to move in some direction – so he identified an area where he could develop.

Hungry and keen to do better, he felt if he could strengthen his self-belief, he would be able to close deals with clients more quickly.

He believed he was 80% where he wanted to be, but he wanted to secure that extra 20% to hit the 100.

Tom was very open to the idea that he needed to work on his inner self to affect his outer success. He knew that if he was genuinely more at ease with himself, his verbal and non-verbal communication would improve significantly and he could reap greater rewards both commercially and for his career in the company for which he was employed.

As we discussed his needs, I noticed that Tom frequently used the phrase: "I want to be at ease with myself and show natural confidence." Pointing this out to Tom, I asked him to explain to me what "being at ease and showing more confidence" would mean for him.

To Tom it meant that any anxiety he may feel when meeting clients, especially for the first time, would be reduced and that communication between himself and his clients would flow more naturally and in particular he would be perceived as a confident professional. He felt that this would be of particular relevance especially when cold calling, as this could often be a daunting task.

I demonstrated to Tom how to enter a relaxed state as a technique he could use for himself. I also explained to him how the mind works and why it was essential to be able to enter the alpha brainwave state.

We then moved on to Affirmations and discussed how empowering positive self-talk could be. I emphasised the need for affirmations to be couched in positive language and how important the exact choice of words was.
e.g. rather than "I am not anxious" he should consider "I am at ease". In boosting his confidence Tom was recommended to install "I am freely confident".

Tom worked installing these affirmations "I am at ease" and "I am freely confident" over the next three weeks. At the end of this period I was delighted to hear that Tom's results at work were improving beyond "good" and also that he was feeling greater confidence in himself.

I am sure with such an attitude and a desire to achieve high, Tom will be an exceptional performer in the future.

## CASE STUDY C

## INSTALLING BELIEF IN YOUR BRILLIANCE

Mike was a 42 year old Company Director who came to me to help him increase his self-belief as part of his career development plan.

He explained to me that whilst at work he knew he had the talent to do well on a technical level, he was actually plagued by a damaging self-belief set. He often felt exhausted by trying to put across to others natural self-belief.

The truth was that what he was demonstrating wasn't natural at all; in fact, he was putting on an act **all the time** – no wonder he was drained.

At my first session with him, my diagnosis was that his unconscious mind was not programmed to allow him to communicate with ease and excellence to the managers for whom he was responsible and equally his communication upwards was ok but not brilliant.

What we needed to do was to agree a programme that would support the belief in his brilliance.

My starting point in supporting Mike, was to encourage his mind to see, feel and hear, as vividly as he could, what his behaviour would be like if he was demonstrating belief in himself – naturally. Once he was able to secure a clear image in his mind, I asked him to describe this to me in as much detail as he could; I asked him to do this using the present tense; e.g. rather than saying: "I can see myself smiling" or "I was smiling" or "I think I am smiling." I wanted him to be more positive and direct by describing what he saw as if it were actually happening: "I am smiling." What Mike began doing was talking of success as reality or in other words as though his vision of excellence had arrived.

After he had completed this stage of our work, I then taught him how to induce relaxation for himself, so that he could enter the alpha brainwave state. He accepted that to reprogramme his mind he needed to alter the brainwave pattern so that his unconscious mind could more readily accept positive suggestions.

Once in this state, I repeated to him what he had previously described to me: about what he had seen, heard and how he had felt when he visualised himself projecting self-belief in a natural manner. Using this protocol meant I was speaking directly to his unconscious mind – in this part of the process he reinforced what he had visualised making it move a little closer to reality. It was important that time was taken at this stage in order for his unconscious mind to absorb the scene as a reality. He needed to not just visualise, but to accept himself as a brilliant communicator.

Mike went through this process for himself, daily, over the next seven days.

At our second session, a week later, I helped him to identify underlying beliefs that would support this new brilliance. Mike felt he needed to feel confident, self-assured, calm and motivated. Following this, I helped Mike install the following beliefs:

> I am calm and confident.
> I am motivated.
> I feel self-assured.

Over the next three weeks, Mike worked to reinforce these new beliefs, programming his mind so that he could operate in his personal and professional life with such brilliance.

Finally Mike continued to play the movie of success in his mind along with continued processing of his affirmations. Mike reported that he was noticing week by week significant improvements in the way he presented himself both to those for whom he was responsible, his colleagues, customers and his superiors.

Mike finally attained the position of Managing Director six months after our work together.

## CASE STUDY D

## COMMUNICATION EXCELLENCE

Richard, an Editor on a busy evening newspaper, attended one of my senior manager training programmes that incorporates *You Selling You* and found that what he learned made a huge difference in both his professional and personal life.

He says:

"I've found myself using so many of the lessons from the course. What particularly registered with me and which has already made a dramatic difference at home and in the workplace, is the vital link between the intra-personal and inter-personal skills."

He already saw himself as successful and had built good relationships with his team of senior executives. He enjoyed his job and was confident in his abilities, but like all those who want to develop and be the best they can, he wasn't prepared to sit back on his laurels. He was good, but he wanted excellence.

He found that the advice given on the course helped him to break down the communication process and to gain a thorough understanding of how it worked. This allowed him to consider more effective ways of dealing with people and situations.

He gave me examples of how he had used the training in the workplace.

On one occasion, he had to deal with an incredibly tight deadline which involved the input of a large number of staff. Using relaxation techniques he was able to approach the task feeling calm, confident and in control. He became aware, however, that as the deadline neared, the adrenalin pumping through his body was causing him to pace up and down the editorial floor and he began to bark instructions to his team. "I wanted those pages completed and I wanted them … NOW!" Richard became conscious of how he may be perceived by his staff – although he had felt calm and confident, his behaviour did not show this. He felt he needed to be overtly calm, so he deliberately slowed his pacing, he lowered his voice, made contact with his team by an occasional hand on the shoulder and he asked them how they were doing rather than shouting at them what he wanted. He didn't need to yell what he wanted – they already knew that. As Richard observed his team working hard for him, if he noticed something he wanted changing, rather than order the change, he suggested it e.g. "perhaps this might work better like that."

Richard's change of behaviour resulted in a lessening in negative tension. This created conditions where he and his team could work with energy and a positive, willing attitude. Taking away the wrong kind of tension did not diminish the positive creative energy present.

On another occasion, Richard had to address 30 members of staff after one of them (who none of them other than the culprit was aware of) had played a practical joke that had gone wrong. It was important that he got the tone of the meeting right – after all 29 members of staff were totally innocent and Richard did not want to alienate them. Even the "guilty party" was only guilty of misjudgement. Richard ensured that he planned what he was going to say and how he was going to say it. He was clear about what he wanted to achieve and why. He felt emotionally comfortable with the action he was about to take – he realised that others may display negative emotion at what he was going to say and he wanted to be clear about his own feelings on the matter so he was not distracted from the course he wanted the meeting to take. As part of his preparation, Richard did a relaxation session and installed positive affirmations.

Immediately prior to the meeting, he visualised the meeting progressing as he desired; he set a firm goal in his mind:

he wanted to ensure also that his staff would understand and appreciate the necessity of what he was going to do. He wanted his staff to acknowledge that they had a personal responsibility, but he wanted to do so without demotivating them; he did not want his staff to leave the meeting feeling that they'd been given a kicking.

He structured the meeting into two sections; the first part included the introduction and the "tough" bit: the second part involved building bridges and a final reinforcing message.

Richard even considered his dress for the occasion and decided that formal wear was most appropriate. To start the meeting, Richard waited until everyone had arrived before entering the room himself. His approach was direct, crisp and business like; he wanted his staff to pick up on his mood and prepare themselves emotionally – that this was a serious meeting and that something had gone wrong. To conduct the meeting, Richard decided to stand rather than sit: this was in keeping with the formality and urgency of the situation and reinforced Richard's control over proceedings.

During the meeting, when challenged, Richard stood firm and rather than raise his voice to support his case, he used pauses and allowed silence to underscore what he said. He took care not to be dismissive of others' points and gave others time to speak, but he remained firm in his purpose; he used clear eye contact and open body language. He used the word "we" often to emphasise that his aim was for the team; it also showed that he included himself in the message he was delivering. This helped lighten the mood and created a sense of shared learning. He ended the meeting fairly informally and in a friendly manner: "OK. Thanks a lot guys."

So what was Richard's verdict? "The whole thing went really well. I prepared myself inwardly and my behaviour mirrored this: my posture, gestures, facial expressions, tone of voice, and pace of delivery. After the meeting he replayed the whole event in his head – even though it had gone well. He wanted to assess his performance, to congratulate himself and to also see if there was anything he needed to learn for the future.

Richard was a perfect example of how inner and outer communication variables can work in partnership and deliver excellence.

## CASE STUDY E

## LIFTING YOUR PERSONAL PROFILE

Jackie is a teacher of English in her late twenties and not someone who has needed my help; on the contrary, Jackie has been fortunate to have acquired a positive approach to her career at an early stage. Her recent rapid rise in her field illustrates well the importance of "personal profile."

Jackie found herself in a secure job, in a middle achieving school. She enjoyed her work, but soon got to a point where she felt she wanted to progress; she understood clearly what a job at the next level up, second in department, demanded, and she was in no doubt as to her own ability to fill this post. So she began to look for vacant posts. Jackie also wanted to work in a more prestigious school than she had experienced to date, and again had faith in her own abilities to survive in such an environment.

Looking for opportunities, Jackie saw an advertisement for a different kind of job than the one she had assumed she should apply for. The job was a new post and involved working in more than one school to help raise standards in English in those students who were struggling, but also to help push those very able students to greater challenges and achievements; it was a post that needed someone with good organisational skills, confidence and flexibility – someone who could create and define the role and make an impact. It was a role that offered a higher salary and profile than a second in department post. One of the schools included in the post holder's area was a high achieving school.

Jackie decided to take a risk and apply for the post – even though it was a fixed contract of 3 years and also an unknown quantity.

She knew that securing such a post, not only would she increase her income and status, but she would acquire a breadth of experience that couldn't be gained so quickly though the normal career route. It would also put her in the spotlight. Jackie also knew that this was an opportunity to show what she could do – her idea was that she would make such a positive impression before the contract expired, that new opportunities would open up for her.

She was not wrong.

Once Jackie had secured the post, she made sure she made an impact. Not only this, however, she continued to work for her future development. During the contract, she made sure she was aware of what knowledge and skills education was looking for, for use in the future. She became the "expert" in key areas to do with the delivery of the English curriculum and was soon being asked to deliver presentations to other staff.

Before Jackie's three year contract was up, a more permanent opportunity, to head up a department in the high achieving school, became available. Jackie applied and got the job. Her success at the high profile post, her constant efforts to remain ahead of the game, to network, to impress people and take risks had paid off.

Jackie's success was well earned – it wasn't left to chance; she didn't wait around for others to notice her; she didn't assume that promotion would come to her as a matter of course – she went out and got it.

She raised her profile and got herself noticed.

## **CONCLUSION.**

*You Selling You* is a programme that develops individuals to inspire those with whom they communicate and need to influence. It is by no means an exhaustive manuscript and the processes I have described could take up a book on their own.

It has attempted to give an overview of practical strategies to support individuals to sell themselves in many situations both personal and professional. This includes developing both the internal and external variables comprising mind dissociation, affirmation, installing belief in ones brilliance, communication excellence and raising the personal profile.

For further information and details of the national *You Selling You* seminars visit www.yousellingyou.com and www.hypnobest.co.uk

I hope you have enjoyed this volume.

Steve Miller

# USEFUL CONTACTS AND WEBSITES.

## You Selling You (www.yousellingyou.com)

An organisation set up by the author to promote excellence in both the corporate sector and in providing 1-1 private consultations. It provides professional training and development programmes aligned to the *You Selling You* concept in a number of areas including sales and business development, leadership, presentation skills and public speaking and personal development.

## Hypnobest (www.hypnobest.co.uk)

A specialist, confidential, clinical hypnosis practice providing highly professional 1-1 solutions for professionals and executives in the areas of:-

- smoking cessation
- performance anxiety
- phobia treatments
- panic disorder
- weight control
- confidence and esteem building

## Steve Miller Training (www.stevemillertraining.com)

A widely respected training organisation, delivering professional training programmes throughout the UK and Europe. Programmes include:-

- management development
- inspirational leadership
- sales and business development
- negotiation skills
- training for trainers
- presentation skills
- personal development
- stress management

# BIBLIOGRAPHY.

Cialdini Robert., *Influence: Science and Practice*
Longman, 2003. ISBN 0321188950

Goleman, Daniel. *Emotional Intelligence*
Bantam Books, 2005. ISBN 055338371X

Maltz, Maxwell. *Psycho Cybernetics*
Prentice Hall, 2002. ISBN 0735202850

Stanislavski, Constantin. *An Actor Prepares*
Methuen Publishing Ltd., 1980. ISBN 0413461904

## ABOUT THE AUTHOR.

Steve Miller is a leading authority in developing individuals from all walks of life in understanding and taking action to sell themselves in a variety of personal and professional situations. Running his own business he has worked with a wide range of organisations in both the private and public sectors and has been described as inspiring, flamboyant and results focused.

Over the last 5 years he has worked with a number of professionals engaging their mind so that they believe in themselves to such an extent that they have gone on to achieve great results. As well as working with organizations he runs a 1-1 practice where he combines the application of clinical hypnosis, personal profile and confidence building.

Working with a range of people including business professionals, directors, managers, actors, trainers, entrepreneurs, teachers, sales consultants, nurses, and media specialists to name a few, his vision of building a world of winners continues!

Printed in the United Kingdom
by Lightning Source UK Ltd.
109840UKS00001B/63